MORNINGS WELL SPENT

Melisa Zimmerman

Speir Publishing

We want to hear from you. Please send any comments you have about this book to info@bridgebuildermm.org

BRIDGE
BUILDER

Thank you to the members of my family. My husband Steven, my sons Mark and Levon, their wives, Brianna and Jessica, my beautiful daughter, Mariah, and my life-giving, world-changing grandchildren, Ryker, Grace, Willow, and Coral. My parents, June and Gene Marrow, who live with Jesus now. My brothers, Ezra and Mike, my "bonus" kids, and to all my friends. This book would have never happened if it had not been for the color you added to my life. Every one of you are truly a treasure from heaven in my life.

FOREWORD

Those who spend any time with Melisa understand quickly why she is so aptly dubbed "MamaLisa." She devotes herself to people like no other and is one of the most Spirit-driven people I know. Along with her work for Victory Church and her own ministry she somehow manages to make herself available when you need her. She'll pray for you at the drop of a hat; she will make your favorite meal and gab about your day; she'll turn your tears into laughter and put your anxiety at ease. Melisa is essentially everyone's mama.

I met Melisa a few years ago while working on a graphic design project for a small group's catalog she had put together, but I got to know Melisa when I walked through her Life Coaching sessions. This book was merely an idea when we started, so it was exciting to watch it grow from concept to publication. She would share stories from her life during our sessions long before they made it to these pages, so I feel like had an inside scoop to the whole process. Throughout the book, she illustrates how God's glory is woven into these very moments…these stories…and that He continually uses them for good. It really goes to show how evident God is in our lives. These moments are integral pieces of His story…your moments are integral pieces of His story.

Throughout our talks and time together, it was easy to see that Melisa's passion is for people to honestly experience God's love and that it's really not a difficult thing to do. Melisa taught me that the more time I spend with Him, the more He reveals through my own experiences. It's truly been an eye-opening journey for me to look back at some of the darkest times of my life and realize He was there all along. I've learned that God will meet me anytime, and quite literally, anywhere. I need only be willing to take His hand. He has a beautiful plan crafted specifically for me and I am (and forever will be) immensely loved by Him. I hope that as you read this book, you'll use it to make time for Him and as a reminder that it is time well spent. It is quite simply an act of love and friendship with the One who loves you the most.

Teresa Lang
December, 2016

INTRODUCTION

In the morning, LORD, you hear my voice; in the morning I lay my requests before you and wait expectantly.

Psalm 5:3 (NIV)

For most of my fifty-three years I have been a morning person. It's normal for me. I recognize that this is not the case for most people. In fact, in my house I am the only one. The others prefer to sleep longer and can, on some occasions, wake up grumpy. I generally wake up happy and ready for the day. I have learned over the years that it is in my best interest, and in the best interest of the other people in my life, for me to start my day off with God. I love the coolness of the morning on my patio just encountering the very presence of a true and living God. Having such a strong longing to be in God's presence, I remember the joy I felt when I truly learned that He wanted to meet with me more than I wanted to meet with Him. For many people, hearing from God and encountering His presence is a difficult thing. Honestly, for many years it was the same for me. I heard about people who spent time with God every day and they heard His still small voice as they prayed and worshipped. For years, I felt that most of my prayer time was a one-way street. I spoke, I worshipped, and that was pretty much the end of it. I can't really remember when that changed, but in the last fifteen years or so I have relished the beautiful encounters of experiencing mornings with God. I recognized that God is not mad at me. He is madly in love with me. I am not chasing Him, He is passionately pursuing me. This change of perspective mixed with some faith, opened a door to morning encounters that changed everything about my relationship with Him. I began to believe by faith that He was always interested in sharing time with me. I didn't have to beg to be heard. He wasn't too busy for me and it wasn't a giant sacrifice for Him to join me in the mornings. He longed for me. *"The LORD your God is with you, the Mighty Warrior who saves. He will take great delight in you; in His love He will no longer rebuke you, but will rejoice over you with singing."* Zephaniah 3:17 (NIV).

Of all the things that have had the greatest impact in my life, I would say two things above all have made the most difference in how I live my everyday life. I spend time in God's presence and I spend time in His Word. My son, the pastor, always says, "You don't have to pray all day, you just have to pray every day. You don't have read your Bible all day, but you do have to ready it every day." This is a powerful truth. For many it may be as simple as starting with five minutes a day. Talking to God in the shower. He is perfectly able to be heard over the sound of the water running. For some it may be easiest to spend some time with God in your car on your drive to work. For me, mornings before anyone wakes up is my favorite time. I have a busy life. I'm a wife, mother, grandmother, sister, pastor, marriage and relationship Life Coach, conference speaker, mentor for many young people, and a small group leader, just to name a few. I love my life, but it is definitely a busy one. I don't have a lot of down time. I have learned to manage it pretty well. I have also learned that if I don't start my morning off with my time with God, I struggle to get back to a place where I can give the focused, devoted time to God that I want to give Him. For me, I try my best to keep it a non-negotiable.

This book was birthed out of those times with God in the morning. My best friend, Mary, for years has said, "I am an analogy person." This book should be right up her alley. God has shown me for years that the world and my life are one great big object lesson. He rarely fails to teach me something when I begin to think about my life. My husband Steven's, first book, "Walking with God" is a book written about lessons we learned from God as we walked our dogs. Many people have enjoyed it and this book is of a similar format. There are a couple of ways to enjoy this book. First, you can just pick it up and read it from cover to cover. Because it is written in short story form, you might choose to use each story as a daily devotional. Each story will take only a few minutes to read but will give you some pretty good thoughts to chew on if you want to do it that way. Whatever way you decide to read this book, my prayer is that you will find God's presence so enticing that you choose to make it a vital part of your everyday life.

As you enjoy the stories of my life, begin to examine your life. Let God teach you more about who He is and who He has created you to be through your own personal experiences. Whether your life is a series of good things or maybe an experience of struggle and tragedy, I promise that God is with you. He never left you and He never will. Finding Him in every part of your life tells a story that is uniquely yours. Sharing your story may be just the thing that helps someone else write theirs.

My prayer for you, as you begin this book, is this; may God open your eyes to see His great love. May you find joy and laughter to be the good medicine God calls it.

May you have an increased desire to spend special time with God and most of all, may you begin to see the story of your life as something that is there not only for you, but to be shared with others as an encouragement for them to encounter a loving God.

WHERE DO YOU GO TO FIND GOD?

At this time in my life our house is pretty full. In addition to Steven, my husband, Mariah, our daughter, and me, we have a couple of other super amazing guys living with us. One is in our spare bedroom and one sleeps in our living room (bless his heart, we need a bigger house.) We really are blessed by their presence and I wouldn't change a thing about it. My normal practice is getting up around 5a.m. and spending some time with God. When the weather is nice I generally go out on the patio and pray and worship. When it's not nice outside, I would just stay in the living room. Did I mention I don't always pray quietly? Because the weather was too cold outside one morning for me, I struggled trying to find a place to pray. I have tried my closet (I mean it worked in the movie, the War Room), but it didn't work for me. I can't get up off the floor like I used to be able to. I tried just praying quietly and that didn't work. So, as a last resort, I went into the garage. After all, we do have some extra furniture out there, including a pretty comfortable office chair to sit in. What I have found is that God was more than willing to radically meet with me there. His desire to meet with me is more powerful than my desire to meet with Him. I have had some really amazing encounters with God in my garage. Why am I taking the time to write this? I really feel like someone needs to hear that God is right there with you; in the very place that you find yourself in right now. No matter where you find yourself at this moment, He is there. Just like He was with Paul and Silas in the prison. Acts 16:25-28 *"About midnight Paul and Silas were praying and singing hymns to God, and the other prisoners were listening to them. Suddenly there was such a violent earthquake that the foundations of the prison were shaken. At once all the prison doors flew open, and everyone's chains came loose. The jailer woke up, and when he saw the prison doors open, he drew his sword and was about to kill himself because he thought the prisoners had escaped. But Paul shouted, "Don't harm yourself! We are all here!"* He is passionately pursuing you. He is waiting for you to cry out to Him. You may be saying 'if you could only see where I am now, God isn't coming here.' Well, God wants you to know He is already there, waiting for you to reach out to Him. Right where you are is your place of worship. Don't let this precious time pass you by. God loves you and wants to meet with you. Oh, and by the way, I may just have the most anointed garage in our neighborhood.

Because Inquiring Minds Want to Know.....
Lessons From the Garage

Sitting in the garage this morning I noticed several things. First, it was cooler this morning than yesterday, but I'm a smart girl and I decided to put on warmer clothes to go meet with Jesus. I began like I always do, connecting myself to my worship songs via my iPhone. Its just helps me zone into the presence of God a little better with some amazing worship music. I have my favorites; they stay on repeat most days. As I sat there, I noticed that in the eight years we have lived in our house, we accumulated a serious amount of clutter in our garage. I should make sure to keep my eyes closed when I pray. In the middle of the garage clutter, God decided to teach me another lesson. He has always used the craziest things to teach me something. God spoke to my heart and said, "It's clutter in your life that keeps you from me." I know He didn't really want to talk to me about cleaning the garage. He just told me that often the busyness "clutter" in my life prevented me from giving Him my undivided attention. I have learned over the years that if I am not intentional about setting aside some time for Him in the beginning of my day, I may go through my entire day and never really hear what He wants to say to me. For the past few years I have been working really hard to train myself to know that God is with me all the time. I love that and I have made a practice of acknowledging Him all throughout the day, but my special time in the morning is the best part of my day.

I pose this question to you; 'What is the clutter in your life that you need to clear so that you can have a special encounter with God?' I have a friend who says if it weren't for college football he would never watch TV. He has learned that time with God is priceless and you have to make it a priority. I'm not saying no TV, but for him that was clutter. God's passion for us is immense and His longing to share His thoughts with us is great. Matthew 6:33 says, *"But seek first His kingdom and His righteousness, and all these things will be given to you as well."* Our obedience to put God first and seek Him first brings the blessings we desire. I invite you to de-clutter a place in your life and make it important to spend time with God every day. Encounter the love of God every day. Encounter His presence with your undivided attention. Money back guarantee..... your life will never be the same.

Just a Word of Advice

If you are just starting a journey of spending your mornings with God, I would love to share a few bits of wisdom I have learned from my journey. Before you begin to think everything about this journey is of high spiritual impact, let me share with you some of my experiences. First, prayer is intended to be a time of praise to God and at times, warfare with the devil. The good news is that God is always present and He never sleeps, so anytime of the morning you get up to pray is great with Him. I frequently have a mental image of Him sitting peacefully waiting for me to wake from slumber and begin to have an exchange with him. He gladly welcomes me to the day and smiles as he enjoys the beauty of my serious bed head. He is such a gentleman that He never rushes me to wake up, even though for the most part, by the time my feet hit the floor I'm pretty much wide awake. This is followed by an exchange of good mornings and I'm off to let the dogs out and to start the coffee. At this point in my routine, I grab my headphones and tune in to my favorite worship music of the day. I begin by just allowing my spirit to open up completely to the Holy Spirit. It's the best. Then I begin to pray whatever I feel led by the Holy Spirit to pray. Some mornings are very peaceful, but on some occasions the need to do battle with the devil for me, my family, a friend, or even our nation, comes to the surface. I usually pray as God leads my spirit. This is a beautiful way to spend your morning.

Let me interject an experience that is packed with some wonderful advice. One morning after not having extra people in our house for a while, aside from Steven and Mariah, who live here all the time, we had a house full. We had someone in our guest room and someone else on our couch. This is not uncommon. We frequently have more people living in our house than there actually rooms or closets for. In fact, my office is often transformed into a changing room/closet for an extra person who needs to live with us. Well, on this particular morning, my office had once again been transformed to an office. I was excited about getting to use my office for my prayer space again. My office is however, right between two bedrooms, the one that belongs to Steven and me and the guest room.

On this beautiful morning I was greeted with my usual hello from God. I found my headphones, picked out my favorite worship music, this morning it was Bethel Have It All. I'm busy getting completely lost in the worship, in the presence of God and the battle with the enemy. This goes on for my usual hour or so. I picked up my phone again to see what time it was and I found this text from one of the kids sleeping on the sofa in the living room "I'm so sorry, mom, but could you pray a little quieter? I can't stay asleep and I only have an hour left. I love all of it but just need a little bit more sleep."

At this point in time I have several thoughts that race through my head at the same time. 'Ugh, Melisa, you are so inconsiderate!' The next thoughts in my head are, 'Satan you will not ruin my beautiful morning by making me feel bad about myself!' I should really learn to leave one of my headphones out of my ear so I can judge how loud I am. These lightning-fast thoughts were then followed by, 'oh, wow! I really feel bad for the poor kid in the room on the other side of the wall.' Moral of the story; praying for people is a really good thing. Inviting God's presence to invade every corner of your home is great. Even putting the devil in his proper place is powerful. But doing it at a level that even the people in the next block can hear is probably not the best approach.

Seriously, God is waiting for you in the morning.

Psalm 143:8 says: *"Let the morning bring me word of your unfailing love, for I have put my trust in you. Show me the way I should go, for to you I entrust my life."* (NIV) Psalm 5:3 says: *"In the morning, LORD, you hear my voice; in the morning I lay my requests before you and wait expectantly.* (NIV) I truly believe that God loves the times when we are intentional about hanging out with him. I also believe that the people in my house appreciate me going to God on their behalf every day. I also know they appreciate it when it's not 5:30a.m. and I'm being LOUD!

ALWAYS BE PREPARED

My mom had a magnet on her refrigerator that said "Don't rush me I'm waiting until the last minute." Why do early what you can put off until the last minute has been my motto for a long time in my life. I would always tell people that I worked best under pressure. In college, I could write the best twenty page papers the night before they were due. However, in the middle of those paper-writing sessions I would promise myself that I would never do this again, that the next time I would start early and not put myself in such a time crunch. Well, you guessed it. I never changed. The last paper of my college career was written the night before the good news was that I passed and was able to work as a registered nurse for many years.

I have found that this as a lifestyle is good for most things. However, when it comes to the things of God and building your faith it doesn't really work. Romans 10:7 says, "*So faith comes by hearing, and hearing by the word of God.*" (NASB) Faith is really something that you must work on building and it happens over time as you learn what the word of God has to say about any given situation. Knowing what the Bible says about your current situation can bring a peace when you find yourself in a scary situation or a sad situation. Knowing what the Bible has to say will help you in EVERY situation.

I woke up this morning with the words "be prepared" floating around in my brain. I have learned over time to ask God what He is telling me. He told me there are many ways that we prepare ourselves each day. One of the best ways to prepare for every day is to start it out by spending time with God and reading His word. I have found out that on the days when I do spend time with God and the Bible first thing, I'm more likely to hear Him clearly. My mind is clearer and I have the ability to understand the Bible better because I don't have to work so hard to get my mind off the events of the day and focus on the Word. I also have a better attitude during the day. I have better interactions with people and most of all, I seem to hear what God is saying to me more clearly throughout the rest of the day. Building my faith by hearing God and learning from his Word changes everything about my day. David felt that it was important to spend time with God in the morning. Psalm 5:3 *"In the morning, LORD, you hear my voice; in the morning I lay my requests before you and wait expectantly."* There is something that is so beautiful about laying your requests before God early in the morning and then watching as He answers those requests throughout the day. So I ask you what are you doing with your mornings? Are you enjoying the peaceful presence of a loving God who is awaiting to meet with you when you wake up? If you haven't established a practice of meeting with God in the morning, I encourage you to give it a try. I know that you will be so glad you did. It's the best way to always be prepared for whatever comes your way.

Connecting the Dots

It's funny sometimes how God takes completely unrelated things in your life and then, just like a child's coloring book, He connects the dots to make a beautiful picture. On this day one of my dear friends is standing beside the hospital bed of her husband, who just went through heart bypass surgery. I had been praying with them for several months for complete health and healing of his body. I had even been standing on the passage of scripture in Psalm 51:10 that *"God would create in him a clean heart,"* (NLT) a heart that was free from plaque build-up and his vessels would function perfectly. We still found that he needed medical treatment to bypass the very vessels I had been praying would be clean. Then I found myself in a place of deep compassion for yet another young couple who have been answering the call to be foster parents. Today was the day that they would return a little boy who had been in their home for months to his extended family. This little boy arrived at their home just a couple of weeks after his birth. Later in the day I received word of another couple who begin a journey walking through a cancer diagnosis of the wife's father. While all of these situations are very different, God connected some dots for me and painted the most amazing picture. I want to share that picture with you.

Dot number one, marriage is a beautiful gift from God that allows us to have a partner to walk through life with. Ecclesiastes 4:9-10 says "*two people are better than one, for they can help each other succeed. If one person falls, the other can reach out and help. But someone who falls alone is in real trouble.*" (NLT) Most of the time a husband and wife can depend on each other for help. As the young couple said goodbye to their foster son, they had each other to lean on and to comfort. It is a difficult time for them. I spoke with the husband and he was really struggling, but a few moments later when I spoke with his wife, it was easy to see that her faith was strong and she was able to provide comfort for her husband. It's because of their faith that they will be able to continue to share their hearts and lives with other children who need a safe and loving place to call home. I'm really honored to know them and see the love of God in their hearts.

Dot number two, when our spouse is unable to stand and contend with us, God is always there. Knowing that my friend is standing beside the hospital bed of her husband that she loves so dearly and watching him battle back from a very serious surgery, I'm amazed at her strength. She is unwavering in her faith. It's because of the tried and true relationship she has had with God for many years that she can confidently face any situation her marriage may encounter. By continuing to read in Ecclesiastes 4 you will see in verse 12 the secret she knows so personally, *"A cord of three strands is not quickly broken."* (NLT)

Dot number three, history brings strength. For the couple that is about to embark on a journey of believing for complete healing from cancer, they have history to build their faith. You see, 30 years earlier the husband's mother faced what seemed to be an uphill battle with cancer. After being given a 17% chance of surviving, she lived 20 years' cancer free. History gives us faith to stand on. Those powerful memories of God's faithfulness help us endure when the current battle is difficult.

So what is the portrait God painted for me today? A masterpiece of His courage, His compassion, His faithfulness, and most of all, that no matter what we go through, He provides us with whatever we need for the journey we are on. God's love is completely overwhelming and always enough.

FACE TO FACE

You have heard the old adage a little wisdom is a dangerous thing. Maybe you have heard, they know just enough to be dangerous. In some things these statements may be true. When I was a new nurse, just starting out at the hospital, I realized that there was so much more to learn and that if I got outside my knowledge base I could really hurt someone. Knowing that you don't know everything or that you don't know enough can be crucial. When it comes to the things of God, however, even a little bit of knowledge is powerful.

I grew up a Southern Baptist girl. A small town in western Oklahoma was where I called home. While I had exposure to knowledgeable preachers, a lot of the wisdom they had was completely lost on me. I did learn a few things. I learned that you should write in your Bible. That underlining and highlighting scripture was important. You knew it was a good scripture if you had it highlighted and underlined in three colors. Yes, I learned how to make my Bible a coloring book. What I didn't learn was what too much of those brightly colored passages meant.

Graduating from high school and moving off to college in another small western Oklahoma rural community brought me even more wisdom. Now I learned that I really didn't know very much. Not from bad teaching but from poor learning on my part. I gained a tiny bit more information about church. The information I took away from them was more about how to be religious. I find it interesting that you can sit under people who have great insight and wisdom and still walk away with such a small amount of what you have heard, or in my case, a distorted version of the teaching. Learning to be religious, but not righteous, didn't help make my life better. Let me interject here with one of my favorite life mantras, "We all walk in all the light we have." I can assure you that through my teen years and my young adult years, I carried a penlight.

Fast forward to 1987. I was married with a small, but amazing, son and because of unfortunate circumstances and a lack of wisdom we were jobless and unable to pay our bills. Oklahoma was experiencing the worst oil bust in many years. There were tons of people without jobs and therefore finding a new job was nearly impossible for my husband. About this time my little brother, Mike, and his family, were visiting from Colorado. After having multiple conversations with them about our dilemma, Mike offered the suggestion that we move to Colorado to live with him and his family because jobs were easier to get there. We decided to do that. We did find jobs. They were not great paying jobs, but we did get paychecks regularly. Our car broke down and we had to ride bikes everywhere we went. Just picture us, our son in a child seat on the back of a bike, trying to bring groceries home. It was a sight to behold, I'm sure. We lived in a tiny one-bedroom apartment and we had next to nothing. It was five miles from our apartment to my brother's house where we took our son every day before going to work. Work was for me five miles in the other direction from our house. So round trip to get to work every morning was fifteen miles. For a non-athletic girl like me it was quite a chore. I experienced my first bike wreck in years that summer. Nothing like falling off your bike, scraping up your legs, denting your dignity, and still having to get back up and finish the ride to work. Yes, I called a taxi to take me home from work that day. Humbling to say the least. We would periodically ride to a nearby town to pawn our stuff to get more money. Living in the beautiful foothills of the Rocky Mountains, having to ride a bike everywhere you went, selling your possessions a piece at a time, and living on next to nothing you would think that would have been one of the worst times of my life. It could have been, but it totally wasn't. While I was living a life that was much less than I wanted, and frankly much less than I expected, I actually met God.

For me those three summer months living in Colorado changed everything about who I was and who I knew God to be. I always say God had to strip me of worldly possessions and move me to Colorado so I could actually meet Him. My life was completely altered when I went from religion to relationship. Knowing about God and knowing God are two completely different things. Having the first of many personal and intimate encounters with Him caused my faith to grow exponentially. I felt like Moses did in Exodus when he is leading the children of Israel out of Egypt. Exodus 33:8-11 says: *"And whenever Moses went out to the tent, all the people rose and stood at the entrances to their tents, watching Moses until he entered the tent. As Moses went into the tent, the pillar of cloud would come down and stay at the entrance, while the Lord spoke with Moses. Whenever the people saw the pillar of cloud standing at the entrance to the tent, they all stood and worshiped, each at the entrance to their tent. The Lord would speak to Moses face to face, as one speaks to a friend."* I especially love verse eleven. There is something powerful about meeting God face to

33

face.

Every morning now, I get up and God is there to meet with me. I'm reminded that He doesn't have to come but He always does. He tells me it's His great pleasure to spend time with me. He instructs me in the Bible in ways I can learn. Now when I color in my Bible it's because the Creator of the Universe has actually revealed what the passage means. I call my Bible, the Melisa/God amplified Bible. It's the one treasure that I would go into a burning house to retrieve.

So I'm curious, do you have religion or have you truly encountered God face to face? Do you know His great love for you? Are you His friend? If you can't answer yes to truly knowing God, ask Him to reveal Himself to you today in a real and tangible way. He is not hiding himself from you. He is there to meet you face to face.

Big Blue Campground

As a young child, my family was what some would consider outdoorsy. They loved camping, hunting, fishing, and bird watching. For years I didn't really feel like I fit in. Being the only girl in the family and the only one who didn't really enjoy those things made me feel like I was living in the wrong family at times.

Very early in my life we started taking a vacation to Colorado every year. The trek from Oklahoma to Lake City, Colorado started out in a green Chevy pickup with all five of us in the front. Seatbelts were not even a thought. In fact, I'm not sure the pickup was even equipped with seatbelts. For us, the mom belt was all we needed. You know what the mom belt is, right? It's the automatic arm that is thrown in front of the young child who was sitting or oftentimes standing, in the seat as you blast down the highway at sixty-five to seventy-five miles an hour and have to slam on your brakes to miss hitting whatever is in the road. Those mom belts saved many a life. On these trips you would usually find one or two of us children riding in the seat between our parents and the other one in the floorboard of the pick-up asleep. Sometimes we would get to ride in the back of the pickup in the camper. It was fantastic. Just image one-hundred-degree weather in July, in Oklahoma, no air conditioner, five people in the vinyl front seat of a pickup truck with the windows down. Yep, it was amazing! Just let your mind wonder to what it must have been like traveling the eighteen hours or so with three small kids in a small confined space. I'm sure it was a lesson in endurance for my parents. However, it was their idea, after all. This was long before the addition of technology to cars. Our entertainment came in the form of five off-key singers embracing such great lyrical pieces as "Froggy Went A Courting," "My Favorite Things, and "Do-Re-Mi." Did I mention my mom loved the movie, The Sound of Music? Oh, and I can't forget the always popular hit song, "Dead Skunk in the Middle of the Road." I'm sure we were a sight to behold. After the long drive to the mountains of Colorado we would stop at the local grocery store and get any needed supplies before heading up a very small two-lane dirt road to my family's favorite primitive campground on the top of the mountain, the Big Blue Campground. Did I mention that we always pulled behind us an old, retired army Jeep? Before leaving Oklahoma, my dad would pull the drive shaft on the jeep. I'm not really sure why, but I'm guessing it had something to do with not ruining the Jeep while they were towing it. Somewhere along the very steep road up the mountain, the pickup, which was loaded down with the supplies we would need for two weeks, would need a little extra help to get up the mountain. Dad would stop and replace the drive shaft on the Jeep and mom would drive the pickup while dad would drive the jeep, still attached to the pick up, to help us navigate the steep climb. Arrival at the camp was then followed by two weeks of trout fishing, (I hate fishing), daily hikes into the woods, (I hate hiking), and for entertainment at night we would all pile in the Jeep and drive even farther up the mountain to see if we could spot some deer, birds or maybe even a bear. I was not entertained by this, either. Can you see a pattern happening here? Two glorious weeks, and I'm the only girl besides my mom. I have no one to play dolls with, no one to do girlie things with. I have no one. These two weeks that everyone else seemed to enjoy were not all that fascinating to me at the time. As the years went by, the vacations continued. We eventually upgraded from a shell camper over the back of the pickup bed, to a cab-over camper on the bed of the truck, to a full-fledged motor home. Even with these upgrades, my attitude changed very little. Year after year I lived what I considered the tortured life brought about by the beautiful mountains, pine and aspen tree lined roads, and a sky so blue it defied description. God's amazing creation was completely lost on me.

So why, at this time in my life, did God bring these memories back? During a morning with Him, he showed me all the beauty I had not recognized at the time. In 1 Timothy 6:17 Paul tells Timothy, *"God gives us all things richly to enjoy."* The Bible tells us that God is an omnipresent God. That means no matter where we are God is always with us. So many times I will ask God where he was in any given situation. As God brought back the memory of my childhood vacations, I asked Him where He was and what He thought about them. He showed me that He was riding right beside me and He was really enjoying the entire event. What He said to me next is the moral of this story. God is always with us. He wants us to enjoy where we are on the way to where we are going. If we let Him, He will show us the beauty He has created just for us. I now choose to look for God's fingerprints on every part of my life. I choose to see my life differently now. I never want to miss the beauty He has created for me. Will you do the same? Will you join God on the beautiful journey He calls your life? What are you missing because you are looking at where you are through your eyes and not God's?

DANCING WITH GOD

You have probably heard the quote "Sing like no one is listening. Love like you've never been hurt. Dance like no one's watching, and live like it's heaven on earth." That is actually pretty good advice. Sometimes as Christians we can have a tendency to think that dancing and singing are silly, that they are childlike and that these things are in no way related to our time with God. I used to feel that way a lot and didn't even recognize it. I grew up in a pretty traditional church. It was the kind of tradition that unconsciously celebrated "reverent behavior." Add that to a home where being dignified was reinforced and I found myself in a place where I just didn't know how to have

very much fun with God. If you were to see my time with
God during those days it would have been sitting very
quietly, praying quietly, and reading the word. I rarely
moved at all. I'm sure God heard me, that is if He didn't
fall asleep during our time together. Honestly, it was kind
of a snooze fest and I think the only thing I got out of it
was the opportunity to check the box on my to do list for
spending time with God. Let me interject here, this kind
of time with God is not sinful and if you are a quiet, dignified kind of prayer person and you and God have great
connections using this type of process, then I say if it's not
broken don't fix it. For me, it caused a serious divide
between me and God. Most of the time it would end and I
wouldn't really feel like I had made a real connection with
God. I know that God desires to interact with us. He
wants more than anything to connect with us on every
level. He is a God of fun and enthusiasm. He wants to
share that with us.

2 Samuel 6 tells the story of how David had returned to the house of Obed-Edom to take back the Ark of
the Lord because David had noticed that while the Ark of
the Lord was at Obed-Edom's house Obed-Edom was
blessed. In 2 Samuel 6:12-15 *"Now King David was told,
"The Lord has blessed the household of Obed-Edom and
everything he has, because of the ark of God." So David went to
bring up the ark of God from the house of Obed-Edom to the*

City of David with rejoicing. When those who were carrying the ark of the Lord had taken six steps, he sacrificed a bull and a fattened calf. Wearing a linen ephod, David was dancing before the Lord with all his might, while he and all Israel were bringing up the ark of the Lord with shouts and the sound of trumpets." We see that where the presence of the Lord is, David found joy and began to dance. David's wife, Michal was not all that impressed with David's dancing. She was so upset the Bible says she despised it in her heart. David was not deterred by her at all. In fact in 2 Samuel 6:20-22 we read *When David returned home to bless his household, Michal daughter of Saul came out to meet him and said, "How the king of Israel has distinguished himself today, going around half-naked in full view of the slave girls of his servants as any vulgar fellow would!" David said to Michal, "It was before the Lord, who chose me rather than your father or anyone from his house when he appointed me ruler over the Lord's people Israel —I will celebrate before the Lord. I will become even more undignified than this, and I will be humiliated in my own eyes. But by these slave girls you spoke of, I will be held in honor."* Sometimes when other people see how we choose to worship God they find fault with it and try to put us in a box, just as Michal did with David. I encourage you, don't let them. For me I am often known to dance before the Lord in my robe and pajamas on my patio. Yes, I have a back yard surrounded by a six-foot wooden fence and people rarely see me. I don't have very good rhythm and I would never, by any means, win a dance contest. In fact, many times when I dance in front of my daughter she reminds me just how silly I look. While others may not think it's great, God does. In fact, according to Zephaniah 3:7 *The Lord your God is with you, the Mighty Warrior who saves. He will take great delight in you; in his love he will no longer rebuke you, but will rejoice over you with singing."* So I figure if God is singing over me then it's my great privilege to dance while He sings. Will you join in the dance of love with God? Will you, like David become undignified? Give it a try. God will celebrate with you.

FILTERS

In every life, the individual is defined on some level by their experiences. As you have already discovered by reading this book, my life has been defined by many fun, sad, difficult, and crazy experiences. My guess is your life is no different. In our house we often talk about how the various experiences of our lives affect our present. We call them filters. How we perceive and react to our life situations is filtered by everything that we have experienced and what we believe to be true about God and ourselves. We try to be really aware what the filters in our lives are and how they are causing us to react to any given situation.

My only daughter, Mariah, who frequently refers to herself as the favorite child, is at the time I'm writing this book, twenty years old. She is probably one of the best twenty-year-olds I know at recognizing her filters and not letting them distort her perception of her experiences or who she truly is. Mariah is a child of divorce. She was six years old when my marriage to her father ended. While I will never completely understand what it's like to be a child of divorce, I have worked with many of them as a Marriage and Relationship and Personal Life Coach. Many of them come with a filter we call rejection. For them if they haven't had a really close relationship with one of their parents, they can feel rejected by them. This filter of rejection can shape who they are the rest of their lives if they don't learn to deal with it in a healthy manner. Mariah is no different. While Mariah tries to be aware of how this rejection filter distorts her perception, at times it will occasionally creep in. She is usually very quick to make an adjustment as soon as she recognizes it. I'm super proud of her!

Growing up, I was always plagued by the idea that I was fat. Acquiring this perception of myself at a very young age, it affected how I perceived my life until just a few years ago. I often found myself comparing myself to the petite and ultra-thin people I knew. I let it impact every relationship in my life. I have tried nearly every diet and diet pill known to man. I would like to say that I am an expert at losing weight. I have lost over five hundred pounds in my life. I was the classic yo-yo dieter. I would lose fifty to seventy pounds at a time. My problem was that they always found me again and came back with friends. This filter caused me to believe that I was unacceptable. I believed that people didn't really see the true me, they only focused on the fat me. You could often hear me say "a fluffy person like me should or shouldn't be able to...." Fill in the blank. This filter caused a lot of unnecessary stress in my life.

Your relationship with God is no different. Everyone has a God filter. If your life has been blessed by God and you recognize it, your filter of Him is probably pretty good. However, for many people who have been hurt by the church, had a serious prayer not answered, or maybe had someone close to them die in spite of them praying and asking God to heal them, their God filter is that He is not a good God. Many people fire God when they decide that in a particular situation He didn't come through for them. This is one filter that truly defines who you are for better or for worse. What does your filter say about God? Is it an accurate filter of Him or is it distorted? Ephesians 2:4-5 say: *"But God, being rich in mercy, because of the great love with which he loved us, even when we were dead in our trespasses, made us alive together with Christ—by grace you have been saved."* If your perception of Him is not that He is a God who loves and cares about you, then I encourage you to find someone who can help you repair your God filter. Don't waste another day. Make a change that will make a big difference in your life.

Going All In

As a general rule, there are two kinds of Christ followers. The first are the people who grew up in church and have considered themselves Christians for most of their lives, and then there are the ones who found their relationship with Christ through a very specific encounter. For the second group of people, they will commonly know the exact date, place, and maybe even time, that they gave their heart to Christ. They will often celebrate that day as a second birthday. I love hearing them tell the story of how they encountered Christ. For my husband, Steven, his decision came as an adult. He was raised Catholic, and as a child had been taught about Christ through the church.

However, at age 18, his father passed away from cancer. Steven tells the story of how, at that time, he was not a "good Catholic." He had mental assent that Christ was there but he was not really actively pursuing a relationship with Him. He didn't really expect God to answer his prayers for his father's healing, but he didn't understand why God would not answer the heartfelt prayers of his grandmothers who were "good" Catholic ladies who were always involved in the things of God and church. So, due to what he perceived as God's unwillingness to answer their prayers, he fired God. It was many years later that his friend, Jeff, began to invite him to his weekly Bible study. For many weeks, maybe even months, Jeff would attend Steven's family's Sunday football parties. The crowd would gather and watch the Minnesota Vikings play. Week after week Jeff would invite Steven to his Bible study after Sunday night football and week after week Steven would decline the invitation until one special day in the middle of football season, when God set the stage for a special encounter with Steven. On this Sunday Jeff invited Steven to Bible study and Steven declined until Jeff told him that a retired Minnesota Vikings football player was going to be speaking at the Bible study. With that sweet bait on the hook, Steven was all in. He went to Bible study with Jeff that day. He heard the story of Christ, his heart was open, and he decided to become a Christ follower. He remembers every detail very clearly and even remembers a quote from the football player that spoke very clearly to his heart. That quote "I'm just one beggar showing another beggar where to find bread." That changed everything for Steven. In all honesty that quote is nice, but it really doesn't seem to mean that much to me.

Meet Melisa. Me. I vaguely remember my decision to follow Christ. I was in church most of my life. I don't really remember a time when I didn't want to be a Christian. I do remember getting baptized as a teenager, but I honestly don't remember the specific date or even the specific age when it happened. I think it was around age fourteen or fifteen. I just always have been a Christ follower. My story and Steven's stories are very different but have the same outcome. We are both committed to Jesus as our Savior. We are both committed to sharing our faith, and we are both certain of our eventual home in heaven.

So what does this "going all in" have to do with anything? Good question. Glad you asked. "Going all in" is a term generally associated with gambling. It's that time when you push all your chips to the center of the table and make an all or nothing bet. For people like Steven, who have had a life-changing encounter with Christ, there is rarely a chance that they will be ho-hum in their relationship and pursuit of following Him. Generally speaking, on the day they encountered Christ, they went "all in."

You see, having a big, specific encounter with Christ often makes such a big life-change that they are passionate for the rest of their lives. For people like me, who have "always" been a Christian, we have a tendency to be less fervent in our pursuit and sheer gratitude for the sacrifice of Christ. For those of us who have been Christians most of our lives and haven't ever had that "ah ha" moment the others had, it's easier to take our relationship with Christ for granted.

So which camp would you find yourself in? Revelation 3:16 *So, because you are lukewarm--neither hot nor cold--I am about to spit you out of my mouth.*" God is not impressed with lukewarm "ho hum" Christians. So I ask you are you "all in" or are you "ho hum" when it comes to your relationship with Christ? I remember for years I envied the people who had a specific, life-changing encounter with God. They had usually been at the end of their rope, hanging on by a single thread when God rescued them. They had amazing testimonies of God's intervention and they embraced Him with everything they had and their gratitude for him rescuing them is evident in all they do and say. For me, I often wondered if I even had a testimony. When I would question whether I had a testimony, most of the older Christians in my life would say my testimony was that God had saved me from having to go through something terrible to find Him. That was true.

God had saved me from horrible life experiences and I'm grateful that I heard the Gospel and in my teen years decided to follow Christ. Truth is, it wasn't until I was an adult and had walked through many of the battles of everyday life that I decided to go "all in."

So I ask the question again, "are you living a so-so Christian life or are you 'all in'?" If you find that your relationship with Christ is "ho hum," choose today to go 'all in,' push all your chips to the center of the table, and give God every part of you. Allow Him to invade all the areas of your life. I promise that is a bet you will want to make and you will enjoy winning the whole pot.

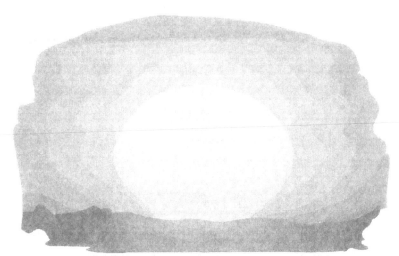

He Will Do It For You Too

When I first met my husband, Steven, he lived in Minneapolis, Minnesota. I lived in a very small town in rural western Oklahoma. I was raised in rural communities and it was my normal. Steven, on the other hand, had grown up a suburban kid. We met on the internet. Our families thought that maybe we were a little crazy, but suffice it to say, God worked it out. I first met Steven in person when I flew to Minneapolis. He picked me up in an older model white Grand Prix. He was such a gentleman. He, of course, carried my luggage to the car for me. Upon arrival at the car, which from the outside, looked like an average car, Steven said, "Let me get that door for you." Honestly, I was so impressed that he was a true gentleman. (He was, and still is today, a very courteous and polite gentleman.) However, in this particular situation, what came next was not what I was expecting. When he said let me get the door, what he meant was that he needed to get in on his side and reach across and open the door from the inside. That's right, the outside door handle was broken. Now I know that you shouldn't judge a book by it's cover, but you also only get one chance to make a good impression. It was December in Minneapolis when I first went to meet Steven. If you know anything about Minnesota in December, you know it's cold. Oftentimes they have their first snow in October and the snow stays on the ground until May. I'm from Oklahoma and I have rarely seen snow stay on the ground for more than a week much less for six consecutive months. Back to the car. What I discovered when I got in the car was even more of an adventure. The car barely had a heater. I noticed an ice scraper on the dash of the car. Little did I know that it would be needed to scrape the ice off the inside of the windshield. The headliner of the car was falling down and to top it off, the blinkers only worked if you manually moved the handle up and down. I am happy to report that the car had a great radio. I was not discouraged because everything else about Steven and my adventure to meet him was amazing!

Fast forward a few months and Steven I decide to get married. He packs up everything he owns and loads the Grand Prix to the top and starts out the drive to Oklahoma. He arrives here in the very same Grand Prix that I had first met him in. I think I forgot to mention the engine was sound. Within a few months we were married. Yes, I got Steven, over nine hundred CDs, and the amazing white Grand Prix. Marriage is a covenant, not a contract and when you marry someone you get all their assets and all their liabilities. I'm not saying that car was a liability, but what I soon found out after he moved to Oklahoma was it also had an air conditioner that worked not even as well as the heater. During the spring in Oklahoma it wasn't too big of a deal and frankly, during the winter in Oklahoma, you could dress a little warmer and make the heater do. However, the summers in Oklahoma can be brutal. Steven found a job in Oklahoma City. That meant that he would have to drive sixty-five miles one way to work every day. In the summer, that is an hour and a half of sweating out all the fluid in your body. He would have to wear a t-shirt and take his dress shirt to change into when he got to the office. Steven never complained. In fact he frequently celebrated that he had purchased that car for only five hundred dollars and he was more than getting his money's worth out of it. The longer he drove the car the more things continued to break on it. Over time, all of the outside door handles broke one by one until the only one that still worked was the back driver's side door. Steven would have to get in the back and crawl over the seat to open the driver's door from the inside to get in the car. Eventually the door to the glove box broke completely off, not to mention the paint on the hood of the car started flaking off. To say that car was not pretty might be the understatement of the day. Steve, though, continued to proudly drive his five hundred dollar, paid for car. He celebrated that his car was not only paid for, but the insurance was cheap and the radio was AWESOME! Given the deterioration rate of the car I was pretty sure that it wouldn't be that long until we would need to replace it. I do have to admit it lasted nearly two more years after his arrival in Oklahoma. During the last six months of the life of his car, Steven and I began to discuss the idea of believing God for a new car. Having done this in the past when I needed a new car, and seeing God do a miracle, I knew it was possible and my faith was high. I told Steven the story of how I prayed for my car and how God brought it just when I needed it and how it as a better car than I expected. So I suggested to Steven that every time he got in his car he should begin to thank God for his new car. He did. We even sowed some seed for the new car, in that we helped other people with their car needs. One day Steven and I talked about him being specific about what kind of car he wanted. Steven decided that he wanted a Buick Le Sabre. To say I was a little shocked by the kind of car he picked might be an understatement. I had never known anyone who drove a Le Sabre that didn't get free coffee on the senior menu at Denny's. But hey, it was his car after all. So I did what all good wives do, I got in agreement with him for his Buick Le Sabre. After all, the Bible says in Matthew 18:19 that *"Again, truly I tell you that if two of you on earth agree about anything they ask for, it will be done for them by my Father in heaven."* So in the power of agreement, we went forth thanking God for the new car. One day we decided that Steven should be very specific in asking for what he wanted. Steven told me that not only did he want a Le Sabre, he wanted a green Le Sabre. So we began to thank God every time we got in the car for Steven's new green Buick Le Sabre. Well, as you might expect, one day while driving down the interstate home from work, the Grand Prix threw a rod. I don't know much about cars but I would soon learn that meant that the Grand Prix had bit the big one. It was toast. Stick a fork in it, it was done. It was now time to get the new car. So we went shopping for a new car. After having looked at a couple of dealerships, we followed my dad's advice to call my cousin's husband who own a car dealership. Sure enough, we called him and told him we were looking for a good used car for Steven and that Steven wanted a bigger car, something like a Buick Le Sabre. Now why we didn't say we were looking for a green Buick Le Sabre, I don't know. Maybe our faith was not as strong as we thought. At any rate, my cousin's husband said he had just traded for a Le Sabre that morning. He recounted that it was owned by a little old lady. She had purchased it from him to start with and he had taken care of the car the entire time she had had it, so he knew it was a good car. Before hanging up the phone, I asked what color the car was, to which he replied, "I don't know, let me go look." He came back to the phone to report, you guessed it, the Le Sabre was green. We knew that we had found Steven's car. So we off we went to the dealership to test drive Steven's new car. We drove it and it was amazing. Leather interior, great radio, all the bells and whistles. After driving it, Steven said there was no way that we were going to get the car for what we had to pay for it. We were paying cash and what we had budgeted was not very much. So we went back in to make the deal on the car. Sure enough, the price quoted was seven hundred dollars more than we had. So we discussed our spending limit with the owner of the dealership, and sure enough he was willing to come down off the price of the car and sell it to us for exactly what we had budgeted. There it was. Steven's name was on his new GREEN BUICK LE SABRE! God was indeed faithful. He had proven Himself to us yet again.

So I ask you, what do you need in your life? Have you built your faith, asked God for what you wanted and then sowed some seed? I believe that if you do these things, in due season, if you don't waiver, you will see God do something amazing. The Bible says in Mark 11:22-25 *"Have faith in God," Jesus answered. "Truly I tell you, if anyone says to this mountain, 'Go, throw yourself into the sea,' and does not doubt in their heart but believes that what they say will happen, it will be done for them. Therefore, I tell you, whatever you ask for in prayer, believe that you have received it, and it will be yours. And when you stand praying, if you hold anything against anyone, forgive them, so that your Father in heaven may forgive you your sins."* It also says in Matthew 19:26 *"Jesus looked at them and said, "With man this is impossible, but with God all things are possible."* So what are you waiting for? Get your faith out and exercise it. He will do it for you too!

I'll Do It Myself

It happens to almost everyone. I have two brothers, Ezra, thirteen months older than I, and Mike, thirteen months younger than I. It was four years after my mother and dad were married before Ezra was born. My mom would always say everyone asked them when they were going to start having children. Finally, in September, four years after they were married, Ezra was born. In October of the next year, here I came, and in November of the third year along came Mike. Mom said people now started asking her when they were going to stop. She always thought that was funny. When mom was pregnant with Mike, everyone started asking if they knew what caused pregnancy and my dad, who was always ready with a corny joke, would just say, "I finally figured it out and I canceled the milkman." I told you it was a corny joke.

The three of us grew up very close. To us it seemed like we were the same age. I'm confident there were many days, having three kids under the age of three, that my parents were probably pretty overwhelmed. My oldest son and his wife had our first grandson, followed less than two years later by twin girls, so I understand how quickly you go from man-to-man to zone defense with kids. In fact, for the first few years of their lives, I wouldn't babysit these kiddos by myself yet my beautiful and multi-talented daughter-in-love seems to do it so easily. I'm sure if you ask her, she wouldn't say it was easy, but she sure does make it look that way. God couldn't have blessed our family any better when He gave us Brianna.

I'm sure two paragraphs in you are now wondering if this is just a nostalgic stroll down memory lane or is there a point to all of this. Yes, I'm getting there, but I have to set the stage first. When I was five years old, I wore my hair with straight bangs, as straight as you can get bangs on a five-year-old galloping horse. It was the time of curlers. For those of you who are too young to remember, curlers are round things with bristles like a brush and you would wind your hair around them and then sleep on them. "Can you say tortured beauty?" If you were lucky, you owned a personal hair dryer that fit over your head that made you look like a man from outer space. Some dryers even looked like you were getting your brains sucked out. They were amazing. On this day, mom had trimmed my bangs and said curlers were placed in my hair to produce the most beautiful, bouncy flipped up curls at the ends of my hair along with a generous amount of poof everywhere else. Maybe one day I will tell you about the curled hair pieces we got to wear to make us look like we had a terrific up-do for special occasions. Back to the story. This day I got my hair done early in the morning because we had an event in the evening. I don't remember what the event was, I was five, after all, but I do remember it was important. Fast forward a few hours and my brother Ezra, being the good big brother he was, decided to help my mom finish my hairstyle. He took me into his bedroom and had me sit. He pulled out scissors I'm sure he snuck from my mom somehow, and promptly cut my hair some more. His idea was to cut only the from the top of my hair, so he did. He cut my hair, curlers and all. What was left was beautiful bangs, bouncy flipped ends and a half inch spike across the top of my head. In his adult life he became a horse trainer, which probably says a lot about how the events transpired when my mom saw his hair cutting skills.

If you are still wondering where this is going, here's the point. Six-year-olds should never cut hair, even though you will hear many stories of kids who do. Ezra didn't have the training he needed to cut hair, he was just doing it himself, and that made him unsuccessful. For many people, planning the path of their life is something they decide to do themselves. Some have more success than others, but the truth is the Bible tells us that every person is born with a purpose, plan, and destiny chosen for them by God. Jeremiah 1:5 say, *"Before I formed you in the womb I knew you, I set you apart, I anointed you as a prophet to the nations."* (NIV) Jeremiah 29:11 says *"I know the plans I have for you, declares the Lord, plans to prosper you and not to harm you, plans to give you hope and a future."* (NIV) These verses tell us that while we can choose our own future, our lives will be much better if we choose to follow the path laid out for us by the Father. What we do with our life and where we go is so much better when we don't choose to do it our own way. So how do you know if you are following God's plan for your life? Start by asking Him. God is not trying to keep it a secret. Look at your life now. What are your passions? What would you do if no one paid you for it? These passions and desires are formed in you before you were born. They were put there by God to help you find His plan for your life. God has an adventure planned for you that will be better than anything you can dream up for yourself. If you are not on God's path today, get there. It will put you on the ride of your life. You don't have to do by yourself.

63

It's In the Book

One of my sons was very inquisitive growing up. He would always ask questions. Many times the questions he asked were very random. When you would give him an answer he would frequently respond with "why?" He was constantly trying to figure out how things work and why they were the way they were. I even remember one time, as a young teenager, that I found him in the kitchen setting a tick on fire. I remember saying "what in the world are you doing?" To which he responded, "I'm burning a tick." My next question was probably the same question you are asking now....."Why?" He promptly informed me it was because he wanted to see what would happen. Then he needed to know why they got hard when they burned? Honestly, I had no answer for that.

These days, of course, I would bust out my trusty smart phone and Google it. Google has answers to almost any question you can ask. The problem with Google is that just because it's on the Internet doesn't mean it's accurate. Most facts are correct, but there are still many stories on the Internet that are not true. Fair warning; be careful when perusing the World Wide Web.

Oftentimes we find ourselves in a place where we really need an answer to a question in our life. It's the really important questions of life that cause most people problems. Why a tick gets hard when you burn it is really trivial compared to most of the questions that people need answers to. What do I do about my teenager that is making wrong decisions? How do I treat my husband who is harsh and sharp with me? How do I know if I should take the job that would cause me to have to move across the country? These questions need real, honest answers and they really need to be answered correctly. For many people the first thing they do is seek the counsel of another person. Maybe they run scenarios in their head trying to figure it out. Perhaps they make a list of pros and cons. While all of these tactics will give you some help to finding the answer to the questions, there is one sure way to find out what you should do. The answer my friend is not blowing in the wind, it's in the book. The Bible is the best answer book on the planet. In it you will find the directions and answers to life's biggest questions. The problem for most people is they have never read it.

The Bible says that every person is created with a purpose, plan, and destiny that is uniquely theirs. God doesn't create us that way and then just send us out into the world without the tools we need to complete the assignment He has given us. He gave us an owner's manual filled with everything we need to know to be successful in this thing called life. One of my favorite scriptures is Proverbs 25:2 *"It is God's privilege to conceal things and the king's privilege to discover them."* You see, God has placed all the answers in the Bible and it's our privilege to find them. Reading the Bible every day helps us find the answers to life's questions. God delights in showing us the answers to our questions in the book He gave the world 2000 years ago. It covers everything from how to receive eternal life to how to treat your parents. It gives great answers on how to be a good wife as well as how to respond to a person who has stolen from you. It teaches how to handle our money and how to choose a church. Whatever questions you may have, the answers are in the book. Read the book. It will change your life.

Keep Your Eyes On Me

Growing up with a brother thirteen months older than I and one thirteen months younger than I was, to say the least, an adventure. I'm sure it was much more adventurous to the children than it was to my mom. My oldest son has three children that are less than two years apart and I know that watching them is sometime like herding cats, so I'm sure my mom had to work hard to keep us all in line, especially when we were little. Simple daily activities become much harder when you have three small children in tow. I remember the trips to the grocery store very clearly. My mom would always give us the obligatory lecture before we exited the car. When we go into the store, you will not touch anything. You will keep your hands to yourself. We are not buying toys or candy, so don't ask. Finally, she would say, "It's your responsibility to keep up with me. I am not going to be keeping up with you." Somehow the idea of getting lost was all it took to keep us connected to her. Honestly, everyone one of us wandered off at least once. I remember clearly my little brother, Mike, getting left on the aisle we had just left. While I know now that my mother always knew where he was, at the time he didn't know that. To say he was terrified was an under-statement. I remember the sound of his voice as he called out for mom. When she allowed him to find her he was scared straight. One unfortunate moment turned into years of him keeping up with mom. Being the busy-body, bossy sister I was, I'm sure that I explained to him how he had violated the directive of our mom and he should have known better. I can't tell you how many times I heard him say, "Melisa, you are not the boss of me." I just like to re-mind my brothers, even to this day, that I never let them miss the school bus and that their lives were better because I was bossy. They might disagree, but you will never know it in this book. Author privilege and all.

No matter how we perceived it, Mom always knew where we were in the stores. She allowed us to discover how much we really needed to pay attention to her. She was always there to swoop in and rescue us, but not without a much-needed life lesson. When I think about how God is a parent to us much like my Mom, I realize that He allows us to go any adventure we want to. He allows us to walk away from Him and do life our way. All the time He has His eyes on us. Psalm 121:5 says, *"The LORD himself watches over you! The LORD stands beside you as your protective shade."* (NLT) No matter where you find yourself, how far you have wondered from Him, God, just like my mom, has His eyes on you. He is watching over you and His there to protect you. All my brother had to do was call out to my mom and she came to get him. All we have to do is call out to God and He will remind us that He has never left us. He hasn't lost us, even though we may have lost Him. Do you recognize that God is right beside you? Have you taken your eyes off Him? It's as simple as calling out His name. He will be right there with you. Our lives are better when we just keep our eyes on Him.

LITTLE CHANGES ADD UP

I am an all or nothing kind of girl. If I'm in, I'm all in. When I decide to go on a diet, it's all or nothing for me. I can't tell you the number of times that I have gone through the kitchen cabinets and cleansed them of anything considered unacceptable to the diet I was about to embark on. My husband is super supportive and he just watches as I rid our kitchen of anything that is not specifically on my current plan. Usually I am successful for a while. Meet Melisa, the typical yo-yo dieter. I usually laugh and tell people I have lost a thousand pounds in my life, however, as I sit here composing this, I am overweight by anyone's standard. My problem, when it comes to dieting, is that I make big changes but they never seem to last forever. The good thing about me, though, is I don't usually quit forever. I will be back on the wagon sooner or later.

In my spiritual life I have learned to take a very different approach. Many years ago I wanted to start developing my relationship with Christ. I had heard so many people talk about their own relationship with Him and it sounded amazing. I had lived a long time with a recognition of Him, but I really didn't know Him. There is a big difference. I started out with my normal all or nothing mindset and thought that if I didn't spend at least an hour on my knees in prayer and an hour reading my Bible every day, I was a failure. I was often unsuccessful at completing my self-invented discipleship plan. That was usually followed by a bout of condemnation. I felt like I wasn't living up to the requirements to be a good Christian. One day someone suggested that maybe I should try starting with a ten-minute prayer time and reading just a few verses each day. All of a sudden I found something that was doable! They also suggested that after a ten-minute prayer time and reading just a few verses that I sit and listen to see if God would say anything to me. This small approach to building my relationship with Christ changed everything. What I found was that this wasn't intimidating and it was so much easier to stick to. Over the years it helped me discover who Christ is and helped me learn to hear His voice. Those two things made me want to increase my time spent with Him, and now, years later, I can easily spend an hour in prayer and an hour studying the Bible. I have a desire to do this several times a day if time permits. Starting small and working your way up can bring about big changes over time. You can't run a marathon on the first day you start running. Building your faith and endurance in your daily time with God is done best when you start small and work your up. The most important thing, if you don't have a prayer time and a Bible study time, is to just get started. Zechariah 4:10 *"Do not despise these small beginnings, for the LORD rejoices to see the work begin,..."* Also remember Romans 8:1 *"Therefore, there is now no condemnation for those who are in Christ Jesus."* How do you eat an elephant? One bite at a time. How do you build a relationship with Jesus? One prayer, one scripture passage at a time. Just get started!

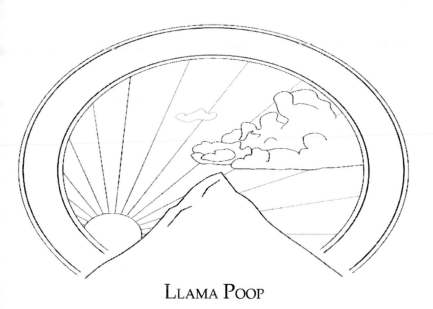

Llama Poop

For many years, my older brother, Ezra lived in Colorado.
During part of his time there he worked on a ranch that
did guided pack trips into the mountains and white water
rafting trips. He learned his love for horses there and that
was the launching pad for his long-time job of teaching
horsemanship and training horses. The ranch was in some
of the most beautiful country God created, the Rocky
Mountains. One thing about the ranch, though, was it was
primitive. By primitive, I mean they didn't have electricity
or running water. They did have solar panels and some
power that way, but that was only in the office. To this
day, I'm not sure why he loved living there so much, but

he did. One of his jobs was to manage the horses. They had around seventy, if my memory serves me correctly. He knew each of the horses, their temperament, and what kind of rider would be best for each one of them. He really does have an amazing gift with horses. He completely understands the language of horses and they understand him, no matter how much time he has spent with them. When we would venture from Oklahoma to Colorado to see him we would always want him to take us on a trail ride into the mountains. I truly believe that Ezra spent some significant time deciding exactly which horse to put each of us on. Because we are family, his approach was different than with the customers at the ranch, I'm certain. On one of our trips to the ranch we were ready to take our traditional ride. Let me just add this little caveat, this is generally the only time I mount a horse. Ezra's expertise is closely equaled to my own inexperience. I grew up with a Shetland pony, but honestly that was way too many years ago to be of much value. Back to the story. Ezra had at this time saddled all the horses. Each selected to accommodate the rider. Whether it was my sixty-something year old dad or my five-year-old son, we all had a horse to ride that would be just perfect for us. Well, almost. For some reason, Ezra thought I needed a horse that was smarter than me. As we road along, I noticed that my horse was busy trying to get me off. He tried to knock me off by going under trees that were too low, he tried to rake me off by riding very close to a fence. All the time my loving brother was busy hollering back at me, "Melisa, who is the boss, you or the horse." Let's be honest, the horse knew much more about what he was doing than I did. A half-hour into the ride we found ourselves in a beautiful meadow when nature began to call. I alerted our guide, my brother, that I needed to find a bush. Ezra pointed out a tree line ahead that he thought would be the perfect place for a little pit stop. I agreed that would work for me. In the meadow there was a large group of llamas. I asked Ezra about them and he said that the ranch was keeping them for some friends. About that time I looked down and saw the largest pile of llama poop I had ever seen. I asked Ezra about it and he said the funny thing about llamas was they use the same place in the pasture to relieve themselves. It was crazy. For some reason I found that very interesting and as I was leaning off the side of my horse in amazement, my loving and considerate horse side stepped right out from under me. Before I knew it, I had an up close and personal view of their bathroom. Good news is I didn't join them in soiling that particular part of the pasture. Everyone in my family thought that was the most hilarious thing they had ever seen. I'm pretty sure that even my horse, that was simply standing there watching me, must have thought it was funny too. So, regaining what was left of my dignity, I again mounted the self-righteous beast and continued the ride. The odd thing was that everywhere we went for the rest of the trip there was some representation of llamas. The Natural History Museum in Denver had a large llama exhibit equipped with actual llama poop. The Denver Zoo has an extensive llama herd. To say I was the frequent butt of the joke told by anyone would be an understatement.

By now you have probably figured out that God can turn even the most ridiculous events of my life into a beautiful object lesson. This one is no different. Life is all about what happens on any given day. Each day is filled with beauty even when the beauty is interrupted by tears or challenges. The question is, what will you do with the day? In Psalms we read that David had many days where he would sing about the goodness of God. Psalm 145:7 says; *"Everyone will share the story of your wonderful goodness; they will sing with joy about your righteousness."* (NLT) This is just one of many passages that convey his joy with the Lord. Before this beautiful praise David lifts to God, he speaks about his unhappiness with God's promptness to rescue him. Psalm 13:1-2; *"How long, O LORD? Will You forget me forever? How long will You hide Your face from me? How long must I wrestle with my thoughts and day after day have sorrow in my heart? How long will my enemy triumph over me?"* (NIV) Just like much of this book, God has something He wants you to know about every part of your life. Whether it's something wonderful or llama poop, let God show you what He wants you to see in every situation. God wants to take you on the ride of your life.

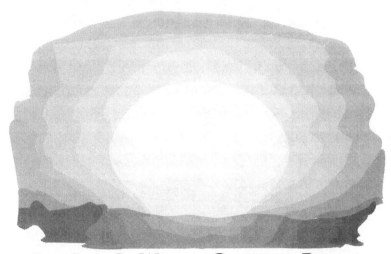

LOU LOU, LAWANDA, GRACIE, OR BRENDA

In our family we have a knack for giving people nicknames. I really don't know why or how it started. My
beautiful daughter, whom I lovingly referred to as "Snuckems" until the age of twelve, when she informed me that
due to the Snookie character on a TV program, I could no
longer call her Snuckems, because I might mistakenly mispronounce it and it could come out as Snookie, a less-than-
savory character on a reality television series. From then
on, her name was changed to Gladys. She loves that name,
by the way. Gladys has since taken on all sorts of vari-
ations. It has been shortened to Gladdy, which actually
represents her personality beautifully. Sometimes, however, I call her Glad, and at times it even turns into Gla-

diola. I almost never refer to her by her given name, Mariah.

My son, Mark, has carried on the tradition of nicknames. His oldest son, Ryker, rarely gets a nickname. Mark has twin girls, Grace and Willow. They, too, rarely get called by their real names. Willow is commonly called Junie, because her middle name is June. She is named after my mother. Then there is Grace Marie. Grace is the one with a plethora of nicknames lovingly given to her by her dad. On any given day she might be Lou Lou, LaWanda, Gracie Lou and recently he has started calling her Brenda. Where the heck Brenda came from remains a complete mystery to me. Funny thing is, both girls know exactly who he is talking to no matter what name he calls them.

For me, I laughingly say my name has been mispronounced so many times that I'm not sure if I'm even saying it correctly. My birth name is Melisa Lei Marrow. Let me help you out with the actual pronunciation of my name. Phonetically it would be MaLeesa Lee Morrow. Yep, I got three names no one can spell or pronounce. That made my life very interesting. I frequently was known as Malissa Lay Marrow (as in bone marrow.) My usual response when people would mispronounce my name was, "I don't know what my parents were smoking when they came up with my name." After all, my brothers have normal names, Ezra and Mike. So really, my parents went way outside the box to choose mine. About a year before my father went to live with Jesus, I asked him who picked out my name. He beamed and told me he did. When I asked him why he chose it, he said, "Because I thought it sounded like dew on a rose." Okay, bet you didn't see that one coming. Me either. It wasn't what I thought of when I said my name, but to my Dad it was beautiful. So I'll take it.

The name a person carries is powerful. It becomes our identity. In the Old Testament, we see names being chosen because of what the name meant or represented. We even notice that at times, God would change people's name because He wanted them to see themselves differently. We see this in Genesis 17:5 *"No longer will you be called Abram; your name will be Abraham, for I have made you a father of many nations."* God didn't want Abram to see himself as "High Father" but rather a "Father of a Multitude." God made this change long before Abraham became a father. He was in his nineties before he fathered his first child. He needed to see himself differently to have faith to become what God had named him. We see this again in Genesis 32:22-31 when Jacob wrestles with an angel all night and walks away with a limp and a new name. Forever after that night Jacob would be known as Israel. Jacob means "holder of the heel or supplanter." This name was given to him because he was born a twin and came out holding the heel of his brother. Israel means "may God prevail." There is so much difference in the meaning of the names when God changes them.

What is your name? What does it say to you about you? What does it say to others about you? For us, Gladdy very aptly describes our daughter because she is one of the most joy filled people you will ever meet. Learning that my name was chosen by my father because it sounded like dew on a rose changed everything I thought about my name and even changed how I perceived my father's thoughts towards me. Most important of all, to me, is the name my heavenly Father calls me. He calls me daughter. He calls me friend. He calls me beloved child. Knowing exactly what name God has chosen for me has forever changed my perspective of myself and how I see my relationship with Him. So I ask again, "what is your name?" No matter your birth name, receive God's name for you. You are beloved. You are child of the King. You are chosen. You were worth dying for. Your name is cherished by the creator of the universe, so live your name.

Never Walk Alone

I have often heard that parenting isn't for the faint of heart. That saying is true. Having grown children, that statement has proven true many times in my life. Watching your children find their own way in life and walk difficult paths without God to guide their way is probably the most difficult of all. Having lived through the years of drug addiction and many other ways my sons used to medicate the pain in their lives was heart wrenching to say the least. Often I felt as if I had caused those wounds. I wanted more than anything to share a love with them that was so big it would immediately heal the wound. Probably next to that is watching my children as they work hard to follow God with all their hearts and still struggle with things that cause the loss of joy in their lives. This is a battle I can't fight for them no matter how badly I want to. Some-times you just have to walk the path to God with the Holy Spirit by your side and allow Him to be the joy and comfort that you desire. Being over fifty, I know that in those times of life, you grow. Actually, you probably grow more than any other time. I try to remind myself, no matter how old you are, there will always be times in life when you struggle with the path that you are on. If you are walking that path with God, then you know the tough things that God allows to happen are there for your benefit and for your growth. Learning to embrace that thought process will help make those times of purpose and power. Where are you right now? Is the path that you are on one that God has designed for you, or is it the path you have chosen for yourself? The two paths have very different outcomes. God's path brings growth and joy. Your path will be only whatever you can make of it on your own. Choose today to find God's path for your life. When you choose God's path, even though there will be obstacles alone the way, you will never travel that path alone but with God. I just want to leave you with a beautiful passage of scripture that will help you no matter where you are at the moment. One of my favorites, Psalm 23. *"The Lord is my shepherd, I lack nothing. He makes me lie down in green pastures, he leads me beside quiet waters, he refreshes my soul. He guides me along the right paths for his name's sake.*

Even though I walk through the darkest valley, I will fear no evil, for you are with me; your rod and your staff, they comfort me. You prepare a table before me in the presence of my enemies. You anoint my head with oil; my cup overflows. Surely your goodness and love will follow me all the days of my life, and I will dwell in the house of the Lord forever."

Oh What a Father

It's funny how every generation feels the need to share with the next generation the incredible hardships they had to endure that the new generation just will never understand. You know the drill, "I walked to school in the snow barefoot, uphill both ways." Yada yada yada. Well, it seems I might have hit that age. It's amazing how much shorter your arms get when you get older. For some reason, which I'm sure came with the curse of the Earth after Adam and Eve ate the fruit provided by the enemy, the older you get the harder it is to see small print up close. So, in an attempt to read, we hold the page further and further away from our face. I always remember people teasing others saying things like, "You want me to hold that for you?" as someone tried to get whatever they were reading just the right distance to be able to read it. My mom, dad, aunts, and uncles shared glasses. At the time of my youth I thought how ridiculous that was. Now, however, I have been known to be out with my close friends and passing glasses around the table just to read a menu. It's true, you know, youth is wasted on the young, but I digress. Oh, for the days when it was safe to walk a mile or so on a dirt road to play with a friend. When I was a small child we lived in the country. My brothers and I were outside all the time. The rule was we had to be home before dark. Our neighborhood, if you could call it that, was really safe. The biggest danger was getting a broken bone, falling out of a tree, or getting poison ivy while playing at the creek. We didn't even know that stranger danger was a thing. Times were simpler then. There were only about six houses on our mile section and everyone knew everyone. Any adult could be called upon in a time of need. Everyone looked out for everyone else. I really have fond memories from those days.

I want to introduce you to Trigger. Trigger was the neighbor's German Shepherd. Trigger must have been a retired police dog. Every kid in the neighborhood knew that Trigger was mean. If his owners were outside and Trigger was not in his pen, you were fine. There was, though, an unwritten rule that you never walked by the Peletty house if Trigger was loose and his owners weren't outside. As a general rule this never happened. I had to walk by Trigger's house on the way to play with my best friend, Stacy. I was always a little bit nervous walking by that house. I was hyper-vigilant as I passed, always scanning the scene looking to find out exactly where Trigger was. Everyone in the neighborhood knew that Trigger had bitten one time before. Kay, the girl who was much older than I, and lived next door, had been bitten by Trigger. It was rumored among the kids in the area that it was because she stepped on him. I wasn't taking any chances. Most times I would just cut through the pasture to go to Stacy's house. Sometimes, though, it was just easier to go down the road. One fateful day I was walking by Trigger's house and noticed that Trigger was not in his pen and his owners were not outside with him either. As fast as a eight-year-old's brain can work, I planned my escape. I would run to climb the fence into the pasture and get away from Trigger before he saw me. Well, as you can imagine, an eight-year-old is no match for a trained attack dog. I was neither sneaky or fast. I started running the ten feet or so to get to the fence and had two hands and one foot on the fence when Trigger got to me. He grabbed me from behind about the waist and latched his giant teeth into my right hip. While I wasn't very fast, I was loud. The screams began and in moments Trigger's owners were there and I was rescued. I sustained a couple of bite wounds that bought me a trip to the emergency room, but it wasn't like I was mauled. I was terrified for many years after that of all big dogs. Once I got home from the hospital with a couple of Band-Aids, my dad took over. I remember Daddy going down to the Paletty's to take care of that dog. I'm not privy to the exact conversation he had with them, but I know it included either they would get rid of the dog or he would. I remember feeling at the time like my daddy would do whatever it took to make sure I was safe. It was the best feeling ever. While my daddy didn't prevent the attack of Trigger, he took measures to make me feel safe again after that.

Today my daddy lives in Heaven with Jesus, but I know that my heavenly Father is just like my earthly dad was. While there may be times that I have to experience difficult or hard times, I know that I'm never alone and that my Father God will take care of me. He will give the things I need to feel safe. In Psalm 91:11 David reminds us, *"For he (God) will command his angels concerning you to guard you in all your ways."* Isaiah 41:10 says, *"So do not fear, for I am with you; do not be dismayed, for I am your God. I will strengthen you and help you; I will uphold you with my righteous right hand."* For all the times I have the opportunity to be afraid or to be worried, these two verses have brought confidence and peace. There really is something about knowing that the Creator of the universe is watching over me every minute of every day. So I ask you, what are you not doing because you are afraid? What would you do if you knew that God was with you, that He was there to guard you in all your ways? I encourage as you read this, decide today that you can go for it. Even if you have go do it afraid, trust your heavenly Father. He is a good, good Father and He takes care of His children. Oh, what a Father!

Parent Fail

Having three children, I'm amazed how all of them growing up in the same environment and having the same parents can be so different. My oldest son, Mark, is type A.
He is always moving and always coming up with big ideas
that he somehow makes happen. Levon, my middle son,
is very laid back. He is gentle, kind, and quiet. Mariah,
my daughter, the baby of the family, is somewhere in
between. She is fun-loving and determined. I often refer to
her as a bucket of joy that sloshes on people. I recognize
that God created them all with their unique personalities,
gifts, and talents so that they will be fully equipped to
complete the call He has placed on their lives. They are all

in the process of doing that.

Levon has always been a low maintenance child. He is very pliable and not much in life ruffles his feathers. From a very young age he was quiet. You often wouldn't even know he was around. He never really made a commotion. Honestly, coming in the birth order after his brother, Mark, who is never missed when he comes in the room, it was quite the change.

I want to share with you what I term as a parent/mom fail. In a lot of ways I'm sure it will shock some of you, make some of you feel better, and depending on your relationship with Christ, might just bring out the judgment in you. By the way, I can tell this story in print now because Levon is over twenty-one and DHS can't come take me to jail. Because Levon was quiet, it was easy to overlook that he was around. When he was nine months old, I lived a block from the church where I served. On this particular Saturday, Mark was at his grandparents' house and my husband and I decided to go work at the church. We gathered what we needed for a couple of hours of uninterrupted prep time for the next children's church service. We had been at the church for about forty-five minutes when I realized.....we had left Levon at home in his crib asleep. As you can imagine, the panic I felt was enormous. I went tearing out of the church and was back home in nothing flat. Levon, true to form, was sitting in his crib happy as a clam and completely un-fazed by being alone. He didn't look like he had been cry-ing. He was just sitting there playing with a toy and smil-ing. Matthew 18:10 says: *"See that you do not despise one of these little ones. For I tell you that their angels in heaven always see the face of my Father in heaven."* I love this scripture be-cause I'm confident that between my parenting and some of Levon's choices in his life, we kept his angels working overtime.

When Levon was twelve, before the time when all children that age had a cell phone, we were going to watch his brother, Mark, play baseball in a large metropolitan city. We were with my mother and father but had driven there in separate cars. After sharing lunch, we were off to the ball field. I arrived at the game a few minutes after my mom and dad. We found our seats in the bleachers and had been at the game about ten minutes when I asked mom, "Did you pay for Levon to get into the game?" To which she replied, "No, he wasn't with us." You guessed it, we had left Levon at the restaurant. Panic once again set in as I drove the twenty minutes back to the restaurant only to find Levon peacefully sitting on the curb waiting for us to realize he was missing and come back after him. To say I was terrified might be an understatement. How did this happen? Well, Levon had in his usual way quietly gone off to the bathroom after he ate. I assumed he was with Mom and Mom assumed he was with me. There you have it, parent fail number two. Don't think for a moment that these are the only two parent fails, there were hundreds. I once heard the quote, "Childhood. It's the thing we spend the rest of our life getting over." Somehow I think that just might be true for my kids.

Telling these stories and sharing my shortcomings as a mom is easy because I know the real truth. God's grace is sufficient to cover my unintended mistakes. How do I know that? Because I have seen Him do it so many times. 2 Corinthians 12:9 *"But he said to me, "My grace is sufficient for you, for my power is made perfect in weakness." Therefore, I will boast all the more gladly about my weaknesses, so that Christ's power may rest on me."* Have you felt alone? Have you felt like you have been forgotten or left behind? Just know that we have a heavenly Father who will never leave us. He promises us in Deuteronomy 31:6; *"Be strong and courageous. Do not be afraid or terrified because of them, for the LORD your God goes with you; he will never leave you nor forsake you."* God loves you. He really does. Let Him be the father that you have always wanted and know that He will never let you down.

REALITY CHECK TIME

When you are writing a book called, "Mornings Well Spent" and it is all about your morning time spent with God, you should probably spend some time with Him in the mornings. Time for a big dose of honesty. I do that ninety percent of the time. My morning routine is to get up around 5:30 a. m. and get my phone with my music on it, my headphones, my Bible, and spend time with God. It always turns out to be the best part of my day. Occasionally, though, my flesh takes control. Either I decide to sleep in, for me that is around seven, or maybe I decide to turn the TV on first thing, or perhaps I get drawn in by the powerful hook of social media. If I allow myself to go there first, I rarely get back to the part of picking up my Bible and finding a quiet place to have a chat with God. I usually feel like Paul did when he wrote in Romans 7:15 *"I do not understand what I do. For what I want to do I do not do, but what I hate I do,"* My question to you is, "What does God think about that?" Many people might answer, God is mad. I believe God is more likely disappointed. You see, He wants to share time with us so much more than we want to spend time with Him.

Growing up, my mom was a person I loved spending time with. She was one of the sweetest ladies you would ever hope to meet. She never said a bad word about anyone. Well, okay, I can think of maybe two people that got on her bad list, but believe me, you had to work hard to do that. I usually tease and say if you asked my mom about the devil she would say something like, "Well, you know, he is always persistent. He never quits. We couple probably stand to be more like that." She just had a knack for seeing the best in everyone. She was never a person to raise her voice or yell at you. If you did something that was wrong, she would tell you that she was sure you did your best, but this time you just didn't make the best choice. If it was really bad, she would also throw in how disappointed she was. That was the WORST! Sometimes I would walk away after hearing that wishing I had just been yelled at or gotten a spanking. I think God is like my mom. He really does see the real us. He sees the goodness in all of us. He knows our heart and is fully acquainted with our hurts and brokenness. He sees our potential. Heck, He is the one who put it in us to start with! He knows what our life could look like if we chose to fully walk and talk with Him every day. So when I say that God is disappointed because I choose social media, TV, or sleep over spending time with Him in the morning, it's just because He knows His favorite thing is to spend time with me. The beautiful similarity between God and my mom is that neither of them punished me or rejected me for disappointing them. They trusted me to make better choices the next time. This kept me from avoiding them later. One of my favorite scriptures is Romans 8:1, *"There is now no condemnation for those who are in Christ."* No matter what you choose, God is not there to condemn you. He is there to welcome you into His presence every time you decide to come. He is there to love you and support you. Never let a bad choice, a mistake, or a bad few days keep you from spending some intentional, focused time with God. He is waiting for you whenever you want choose to join Him. Go see what He has for you today.

SHUT UP AND MARCH

I have a lot of job titles. I am a Co-Founder of Bridge Builder Marriage Ministry, an author, a conference speaker, Life Coach, a teacher, and an administrator for the ministry. I also work at Victory Church in Oklahoma City as an Associate Pastor. In that role, I am in charge of all our small groups. Wearing a lot of hats and moving from one role to another is not really that hard for me. I am geared to be a great multi-tasker. In fact, I would say it is what keeps me from getting bored with my life.

At Victory Church one of the normal things we do is to have many of our Small Groups in our building. The majority of them are Sunday morning. Because Victory is a large church, we have multiple worship experiences on Sunday morning. We also have a building that is large enough to have a lot of classrooms where Small Groups can meet. It works great for our groups because it provides two things. First, it allows people to attend a group and attend a worship experience on the same day so that it is not adding another days event to their already busy schedule. It also provides childcare for people in our groups because we allow children to attend our Children's Church for two services. We have the most amazing Children's Pastors ever! Most kids are thrilled to get to stay in Children's Church for two worship experiences. Back to the point of this, as the Small Groups pastor, one of my jobs is to schedule the rooms for the Small Groups that want to meet in the building. Honestly, this is like a giant jigsaw puzzle. The thing that makes this job difficult, at times, is that I have to coordinate the Small Group rooms with everything else going on in the building, which might include Freedom Classes, Equip Classes, Training Sessions, and Youth events. The list goes on and on. We do have a software program that helps with this, but it still seems like if you move one class, you have to move four more to make it work. It's harder than it sounds to make sure everyone has the room they need, at the time they need it, and it's a room that is not too big or too small for the size of their group. I have spent several hours rearranging groups to accommodate one simple change in someone's group or another department's event. Why you needed to know all of this is about to become clear.

I recently had a dream, which I believe was from God. God spoke to many people in dreams and visions in the Bible and I'm glad He speaks to me that way sometimes, too. In my dream I was acting in my role as Small Group Leader of a Pre-Marriage group. This is a group, that in my real life, I have often led. My group had been scheduled to happen in a large open room. The group started off small, but people kept coming and the group got larger and larger. There was a lot of commotion going on in the areas around the place where the group was supposed to be meeting. So I decided to move our group to a closed-in room because people were having trouble hearing me while I was teaching. I set off to take my group to a different room. When I got to the next room, where I planned to have my group, someone was already using it. This happened with the next two rooms I went to. What I noticed was that as I had to move from one room to the next, people kept either getting lost or quit following me. The ones who did follow me started to complain about having to constantly move from one room to another. It was becoming stressful to try and make this all work out. I woke up and asked God what the dream meant. This is what He told me. First, He reminded me about the children of Israel marching around the wall at Jericho. In Joshua, chapter six, it tells the story of how God directed Joshua to lead the Israelites around the city of Jericho one time every day for six days and on the seventh day they were to march around the city seven times. On the seventh lap around the city, when Joshua gave the signal, everyone was to give a great shout and the walls would come tumbling down. One interesting part of the story is that the people were to keep silent on their laps around the city until the last lap. Having worked with groups of people for a long time, I have found that in any group of size, there are usually people who complain about what you are doing, how you are doing it, where you are doing it, and the list of complaints goes on and on. I can just imagine, as the people marched around the entire city day after day, there was a great opportunity for them to complain, "My feet are killing me." "Who does Joshua think he is making us march around the city every day?" "It's too hot out here for us to be marching around this entire city." There was probably no end to the list of complaints that could be made, yet the instruction they had was to not say a word and continue to march. I'm sure that there must have been times when Joshua would have to look at them and say, "Shut up and march." In my dream the people had trouble just following me where I was leading. They either dropped out or continued to follow and complain. When I asked God about the dream, this is what He said to me. He said, "When you choose to follow the path I have laid out for you and obey what I tell you to do along the way, you have success. When you choose to leave the path or complain that the path is too hard, you miss the very thing I am trying to give you or the place I am trying to take you." Then I remembered something I heard renowned teacher/speaker, Joyce Meyer say, "You can be pitiful or powerful, but you can't be both." My dream began to make sense. What are we missing because we don't want to take the path that God has for us? What battle are we losing because we don't' want to fight the way God directs us to fight? Marching around a city with your mouth shut for seven days and then marching around seven times on the seventh day and then shouting doesn't sound like the best battle plan ever. Isaiah 55:8-9 *"For My thoughts are not your thoughts, nor are your ways My ways," declares the LORD. "For as the heavens are higher than the earth, so are My ways higher than your ways and My thoughts than your thoughts."* God really does know best. He has our best interests at heart. Are you choosing to follow God or do you just need to be reminded to just shut up and march?

SLEEP VERSUS SLUMBER

I'm not a person who likes to just lounge in bed for long hours. I want to go to bed when I'm sleepy and get out of bed when I'm awake. I have always been that way. I have a friend who would enjoy sleeping until noon every day if she had that luxury. For the life of me I can't figure out why. So getting up early in the morning when it's still dark outside is a usual part of my life. I don't mind it all. Most times I look forward to my morning time with God. However, 4:15am or 4:30am is not really something that even I, the morning person, enjoys. As a general rule when I find myself in a pattern of waking up before my customary 5am, I toss and turn and tell myself, "it's too early to get up." I'm not sure why I think that thirty additional minutes of sleep will make that much difference in my day anyway.

This morning was one of those mornings where I really didn't want to get up at 4:15am. I tried going back to sleep and woke back up promptly at 4:30am. This time a verse flashed through my mind. Psalm 121:1-3 says *"I will lift up my eyes to the mountains; from where shall my help come? My help comes from the Lord, Who made heaven and earth. He will not allow your foot to slip; He who keeps you will not slumber."* He is watching over me, just like I have so often spent time in the night watching lovingly over my children as they sleep. So no matter what time of the morning I wake up, I never have to wait for God to wake up to spend some beautiful time in the morning with Him.

This is totally unrelated, but my mind went there, so I'm going to share it with you to add some humor to your life. When my middle son, Levon was a very small boy, we had a friend, Kenneth Dobbs. Kenneth enjoyed teasing Levon by using words that he didn't understand. Some of his frequent questions to Levon were, "Do you slumber in the bed?" Levon was always very adamant that he did NOT slumber in the bed! Kenneth would then ask him, "Well, do you have garments on your back?" Once again Levon would definitely assure him he did not. This would then finally be followed up with Kenneth saying,

"Well, I bet you have forefathers." Levon, true to form, would continue his defense that he only had one father. This game was one that Kenneth delighted in and Levon was frustrated by. Sometimes picking on small boys is just fun. What fun memories God brings to mind from time to time. Just another reason I love God. He is, after all, a father that passionately loves us and wants us to enjoy our lives. Check out John 10:10 in the amplified Bible if you need proof of that statement.

Ok, now to tie up the loose ends. We have a very relational Heavenly Father who is always longing to spend time with us. He patiently and lovingly watches over us when we sleep and eagerly awaits our waking up. He wants to share every moment of the day with us, but I really believe His favorite time of the day is when we are alone with Him and He has our undivided attention. This purposeful time with God will indeed be time well spent.

THE APPLE AND THE TREE

I'm pretty sure you have heard the saying, ' the apple doesn't fall too far from the tree. ' In many cases that is very true for me. I loved my dad. He was hard working, handsome, and a man who was friends with a lot of people. Growing up, all my friends loved him. I loved my dad all my life. That doesn't mean that we always had a great relationship. My dad was very driven towards success. He was always a part of the important things going on in the small town I grew up in. The public side of my dad was the picture of success. However, keeping up that kind of an exterior appearance is hard work. What I didn't know until conversations with my dad late in his life, was that he never felt he got the approval of his father. He never felt like his dad was proud of him. He was driven by the need for approval. People filled that need for him.

Most of his worth and value was tied up in what other people thought of him. His success was dictated to him, not by his own satisfaction in his accomplishments, but more so in the accolades of others. This insecurity didn't make him less valuable, less of a dad, but it did make him driven and insecure. I loved my dad.

Here is where I come into the picture. Our choices, our personal struggles, and our beliefs have an impact on the people closest to us. The description of my dad all too often describes me as well. While I am very aware of my need for validation from people, and yes, I recognize this is not healthy and I am intentionally working to change that in my life, I'm still a work in progress. People in the church world would call this a generational curse. How do I deal with this? First I take it to the Word of God. In the Bible I read in Colossians 3:13 *"Christ redeemed us from the curse of the Law, having become a curse for us-- for it is written, "CURSED IS EVERYONE WHO HANGS ON A TREE."* (NASB) Jesus paid the price so I don't have to continue to struggle with the same things my dad struggled with. I can live free from it. Galatians 5:1 says, *"It was for freedom that Christ set us free; therefore keep standing firm and do not be subject again to a yoke of slavery."* (NASB) I can live free from the need for people to provide approval for me. Next, I change my internal dialog. I begin to take a real look at what I am actually telling myself. For years I have asked myself this one question, "What would my life have looked like if someone had validated the call of God on my life when I was fifteen, when I recognized it myself?" That question in itself is very telling of the fact that the need for people's approval had successfully transferred from my dad to me. I would love to tell you that I have eradicated that lie from the things I tell myself. The truth is that it is a battle that I still fight from time to time. I have to continue to take myself back to the Word of God and remind myself that God accepts me and validates me and has called me His very own child. He validated me when He sent Jesus to die on the cross for me. He accepts me just the way I am and He has made me a new creature in Christ the moment I accepted Him. That validation is more than enough for me. I remind myself that I see myself differently than most people see me. My harsh evaluation of myself is often much more severe than that of others. Most of all, I remind myself that God's view of me is the single most important view of me and I must come into agreement with who He says I am. Today I choose to do just that.

What tree did your apple fall near? What does your internal dialog say about you? Maybe my struggle will resonate with you. If so, I encourage you to change what you tell yourself, identify yourself with what God says you are, and watch as you become set free to be the amazing person you are truly created to be. Did I mention I love my dad?

THE BEST FAMILY EVER

Families are funny things. Some conjure up memories of great times, fun, and closeness while others provide memories of pain, sadness, or maybe even isolation. For me, the first is more accurate. Both my parents came from families with six kids. While my mom was the oldest, my dad was the youngest son and the next to the youngest child. In fact, his oldest brother was twenty years older than him. My mom's family, while close, was not one that we grew up going to see every Sunday, as we did my dad'-s, even though they lived in the same town. My dad's family was very connected and it was the standard expectation that all members of the family would be there when they got together. I remember even into my young adult life, that when I heard the Marrow's were getting together you were expected to go, period. When you went you brought some type of food, which, by the way, was never said but was an unwritten rule. Growing up with this standard it was an easy fit for me. I grew up loving this big family experience. Some of my best memories are from my early childhood, when nearly forty people would cram into my Grannie Marrow's small, two bedroom frame house, which must have been about twelve hundred square feet and we would eat lunch and play. We always had more than enough food. It was an unwritten rule that it was not a family meal unless Grannie made cinnamon rolls, chocolate pie, coconut pie, egg custard pie and Aunt Guynel made Scotch-a-roos. There were several other things that people usually brought, but these were ALWAYS a must. We would eat until we were over-full, then the games would start. We would have the domino table where there was frequently loud domino slamming on the table followed by great rounds of laughter as someone made the great play, not to mention the common phrase, "high, low, jack, game" which was, of course, what the winner of the pitch card game would say. Funny, I never learned to play pitch because that was an adult game. There was also the group who were busy yelling at the television as they watched the weekly football game. We were a LOUD family for sure. It wasn't uncommon for someone to trick someone else into going to the phone or going to check on the kids just to get their chair. In a house that small with that many people, chairs were at a premium. All these things took place as thirteen grandchildren and six great-grandchildren played on the screened-in front porch. It was really a great childhood. With both of my parents living with Jesus now, I love remembering and I long for the days of my childhood.

As a grandmother now, I wish that my family still had that tradition of coming to "Lovie and Poppy's" house every Sunday, but our life is different. Because I am a pastor, Mark, my oldest son, who is a pastor of a church in a different town, Levon, our middle son, is on the worship team of still another church, it's hard to get us all together on Sunday. Our daughter, Mariah, is on the worship team at the church where I pastor and she still lives at home so she frequently joins Steven and me for Sunday lunch, but it is far short of the eleven we would have if everyone came. I would trade Sunday's at Lovie and Poppy's house for all my children being in the ministry and leading people to Christ every day.

What I can say is this. While my family is not nearly as large as my mom and dad's families were, God has brought so many other people into my life that I all call family. I have "bonus" kids who call me mom and Steven dad and show up frequently at my house. Bonus kids are kids that aren't near their parents or don't have parents, who have more or less adopted Steven and me as their parents away from home. God has also blessed me with four couples that I do life with on a very regular basis who are like sisters and brothers to me. They are bonus aunts and uncles for our daughter, Mariah. In fact, recently we were together celebrating a birthday when the discussion of us becoming old came up and how we would expect Mariah to take care of all of us. It was so hilarious that we even face timed her to just make sure that she knew of her expected role. She was fully aware and completely on board.

Maybe you find yourself in a place where you are without birth family or even bonus family. That is difficult for sure, but the Bible says in Psalm 68:6 "God sets the lonely in families." (NIV) 1 John 3:1 says *"See what kind of love the Father has given to us, that we should be called children of God; and so we are. The reason why the world does not know us is that it did not know him. Beloved, we are God's children now..."* (EXV) When you become a child of God by surrendering your heart to Him, you become part of the family of God. You are joining brothers and sisters in the best family in the world. The good news is that the best family in the world still gets together every Sunday at Father God's house for fellowship and fun. My question to you is, are you missing the family get-togethers or are you there bringing what only you can bring that makes the family whole? If not, join the family, come and engage, celebrate the best family ever.

THE MIND! IT'S A TERRIBLE THING TO WASTE

"The mind, it's a terrible thing to waste." This quote from years ago somehow found its way back into my mind this morning. Not necessarily a bad thing, right? Unless it is right in the middle of your prayer time. In the words of my daughter, "What the mess?" I love being intentional about recognizing the presence of God. Praying in the morning is truly one of the times I feel most connected to God's presence. So why, then, do ridiculous random thoughts dart through my brain like a wild teenager cruising the Autobahn? I'm not sure I have an answer for that. Today those thoughts included, 'I wonder what the balance is in my checking account? Oh, wait, I have three of them...do

any of them have money left?' Followed by the list of what
I needed to purchase for Thanksgiving. 'Do I know if anyone is coming to Thanksgiving at my house on Thursday?'
I should make some calls and find out. We really need to
do family pictures at our family Thanksgiving, we now
have Coral, our fourth grandchild. The truth is, there are
times when I don't have so many random thoughts going
through my head when I pray, but today just wasn't one of
those days. What's a girl to do? Over the years I have
learned a couple of techniques that help. First of all, I don't
get too upset that it happens. I figure God is big enough to
roll with the flow. I sometimes will jot down on a piece of
paper the things I need to take care of. Other times, I will
just ask God to remind me of them later. There is no loss in
the closeness of God when my mind seems to wonder. He
is still there. He still loves me and most of all, He isn't upset with me. The beauty of this morning was that God reminded me that He fully understands me and yes, that in-
cludes my ridiculous rabbit trail thoughts. He reminds of
Jeremiah 1:5 *"Before I formed you in the womb I knew you, before you were born I set you apart;"* He reminded me that
spending time with me is one of His biggest delights no
matter what my brain is doing. Most of all He reminds me
that I am one of His favorite kids. What a treasure to know
that the Creator of the universe loves me. He loves you,
too. You are one of His favorite kids. I encourage you

today to make some time to spend with the One who loves you the most. God. His presence is a terrible thing to waste.

THE WORLD IS A STAGE

My beautiful granddaughter, Grace Marie, is such a joy! At age three she is an amazing worshipper of God. She loves to sing worship songs and loves to pretend to play the piano. She has done this from a very young age. It's easy to see what Jesus meant when He told the disciples, *"Truly I tell you, unless you change and become like little children, you will never enter the kingdom of heaven"* in Matthew 18:3. For us, though, Grace very much celebrates the great introduction of her upcoming performance and will be very quick to let you know that she will be taking the stage. She expects that everyone will give her their undivided attention and will loudly celebrate the arrival of the princess to sing. In fact, recently her older brother was outside with Poppy (the name chosen for my husband)

and they could hear the loud announcement for the princess' upcoming song. Their conversation went something like this, Poppy: "Did you hear the announcement for Grace to take the stage?" Ryker: "Yes I did, for like the fourteen hundredth time." Big brother is much less interested in Grace's performance than everyone else. When Grace takes the stage it is done with a very dramatic entrance, complete with bows, twirls, and raised hands. You will never miss her entrance. She will repeat this glorious entrance over and over and over as long as anyone will announce her coming. As a grandmother, I'm happy to indulge her any time she wants me too.

God used all this performing to spark a thought. He asked me, "Do you need a stage to do what I have called you to do?" Excuse me while I take a minute and minister to my bruised ego. If I am completely honest, I do enjoy the accolades of others. Mostly, I love when people compliment me on tasks I have completed. There is something powerful about the validation of others. While this is not always bad, to live our life based on the need for someone else's approval is a bad place to be. I know so many people whose worth and value is completely tied up in what other people think of them. It's this viewpoint that makes life difficult for many. I have struggled for many years wondering what it would have been like if someone had validated the call of God on my life when I recognized it at age fifteen. It wasn't until late in my adult life that God opened the door for me to fulfill that call in a public way. Now I wonder what I lost because I was waiting on someone else's approval when I had the approval of God all along. Maybe you find yourself in the place where other people's voices are very loud in your life. To quote Jennie Mayo, "If God assigns you He can find you." Your willingness to follow God and do what He has called you to do must never be based on whether any other person sees the greatness in you or not. Your greatness is a gift from the Father and His desire is for you to live it out in living color. James 1:7 says, *"Every good and perfect gift is from above, coming down from the Father of the heavenly lights, who does not change like shifting shadows."* Your gift is one given to you by God and He wants so much for you to live out the gift. Make the stage of your life be for an audience of one. Revel in the adoration and applause of the Creator of the Universe. His is the opinion that matters most, so take the stage with a twirl and a bow. God is waiting.

THINGS IN THE DARK

As a very small child I lived in the country. By the country I mean we lived seven miles out of town, the roads were dirt and our house was surrounded by pasture. There were only four houses on our mile section. Our property included five acres. It was a great time in life. The simple things were the best. It was a time when a child could play outside all day and as long as you came when mom honked the horn of the pick up three times or you were in the house by dark, it was fine. We didn't think much about crime and the biggest fear in our lives came from falling out of a tree or getting hurt jumping our bikes over homemade ramps. Times really were simpler then.

Somehow, though, I didn't escape fear altogether. There was always the fear of what happened in the dark. One of the perks of being the only girl in a family of five was that you got your own bedroom. My brothers, Mike and Ezra had to share a room. I, of course, got my very own bedroom. You would think a girl would find this benefit one of sheer joy. I did most, of the time....except at night. I didn't have the benefit of having someone to sleep in the room with me. My bedroom had a double window to the front porch. It let in great light, but that meant that the boogie man had access to me during the dark much easier, right? I'm not quite sure where this fear came from, and honestly, ninety percent of the time it didn't even come around. However, the ten percent of the time it did, it was terrifying. Often when it happened, I would do one of two things. I would either violate the rule my parents had about no children sleeping in their bedroom by slinking stealthily into their bedroom and sleeping on the floor at the foot of their bed, hoping to wake up before they did and return unnoticed to my own bed. Sometimes I would just go join one of my brothers in their bed. They didn't really like it, but they weren't able to dole out punishment like my parents might. There was something very comforting about knowing that I was not alone. When you are five or six years old, things that go bump in the night are not a welcome visitor. Occasionally throughout the years of my childhood, I would somehow talk my older brother into taking my bedroom and I would get the privilege of moving into the bedroom with my little brother. I'm sure my brother thought my fear had won him the bedroom lottery. Fortunately, I grew out of that fear. I'm now perfectly fine to sleep in a bedroom by myself. I mean, really, how awkward would it be if I still entertained that fear at fifty-plus years of age?

Fear is a very real thing. There are many forms that fear can take in a person's life. For most people, fear is something that can be managed. For some, however, fear can be debilitating. Learning to overcome fear brings freedom. As I learned to feel safe in my own bedroom, I no longer had to violate family rules or slip into the bed of my brother. I was able to enjoy a peaceful night's sleep. Unless there has been trauma associated with the dark, that fear is, for the most part, something that can be left in one's childhood. Other fears can stay with us for life. One thing I have learned about fear is that by using the power of the Word of God and the presence of the Holy Spirit you can overcome them. We are reminded in John 14:27 *"Peace I leave with you; my peace I give you. I do not give to you as the world gives. Do not let your hearts be troubled and do not be afraid."* God has a beautiful way of exchanging fear for peace in our hearts when we learn to trust Him. Psalm 34:4 *"I sought the LORD, and he answered me; he delivered me from all my fears."* Yet another promise that God has provided a way for us to live a life free of fear. So what fear are you holding on to? What is it that you need to give to God? Always remember 2 Timothy 1:7 " For God hath not given us the spirit of fear; but of power, and of love, and of a sound mind." (KJV) You can live a life free from fear. It's the life that God has provided. All you have to do is walk it. It may not happen overnight, but as you renew your mind to the Word, you will see your life change. What are you waiting for?

This Present Moment

As a young adult, my mom gave me a piece of advice. She would say, "Melisa, if you can't get up, fix breakfast, get your house picked up, get your kids off to school, and be at work by eight, it is just because you are not organized." She was speaking from experience. She did it every day. In fact, I have two brothers, one thirteen months older than I and one thirteen months younger than I. We were never late for school and my mother, was to my knowledge, never late for work. As a young mom I marveled at how she made that happen every day of my life. Now I know it was because she never slept late. By sleeping late, I mean past five in the morning. Maybe that is why I, too, am a morning person. Perhaps it's genetics or maybe it's environmentally learned. Either way, I know that if you start your day early enough, you can complete a ton of tasks before it's time to go to work.

Why is this story important, you ask? As a young person, I thought that sleep was super valuable and you should try and get as much as you could every night. While there may be some truth to that, there are some things that are more important. For years if I woke up in the middle of the night I would be upset about having my precious sleep interrupted. As I grew older I learned it might not always be such a bad thing. Some things happen only when you do not have to give your attention to multiple tasks at the same time. For instance, I had the best conversations with my children in the middle of the night. It was their time to talk. They had my undivided attention. I remember one time my husband, Steven, said "Why can't they talk to you during the day?" My only answer to that was, "While it would be more convenient, I'm not willing to risk them not talking to me at all. So if they want to talk at two in the morning, it's valuable enough for me to get up and listen." He saw the logic in it and never asked that question again. In fact, if they wanted to talk to him, he would get up and talk to them in the middle of the night, too, and he was never bothered by it. For me this would become the training I needed for waking up to listen to God speak. Learning not to be upset because my kids would wake me up to talk helped me better understand the importance of God waking me up to talk. For years now, I have made it a practice of asking God what He would like to say to me when I wake up in the middle of the night. Today He said to me, "This present moment is someplace I want you to learn to live." James 4:13-15 reminds us, *"Come now, you who say, "Today or tomorrow we will go to such and such a city, and spend a year there and engage in business and make a profit." Yet you do not know what your life will be like tomorrow. You are just a vapor that appears for a little while and then vanishes away. Instead, you ought to say, "If the Lord wills, we will live and also do this or that."* Embracing living in the present is very powerful. Learning to live my life that way is a game changer. All too often instead of focusing on the present moment, my mind is focused on two hours from now or two days from now or something in the past. That focus shifts my attention from the beautiful thing God wants to do in this present moment. God speaks clearest when my attention is on the present moment. So at three in the morning, when I wake up, I have learned the art of focusing on the present moment. What does God want to say, what do I need to do? What treasure is in this present moment? What would happen if we all decided to live in this present moment?

THREE FATHERS

I have three kids and they have three fathers. You see I'm a part of the crowd who is divorced and remarried. When my children were six, twelve, and sixteen they received the gift of a bonus dad. We refer to my husband, Steven, as a bonus dad. We chose bonus instead of step-dad because steps are something that get walked on and bonus is something that you get in addition too. Fortunately, all my children have a good relationship with their biological dad. Steven always says his family came pre-assembled. So, of course, the third dad is the best dad of all, God.

In our family all my children look different from each other. Mark, my oldest son, sometimes looks a lot like my dad, but sometimes I see his dad in him, too. Levon, my middle son, looks exactly like my oldest brother. It definitely looks like he was born to the wrong sibling. He is my brother from the way he looks, to the way he talks, to his personality. Really, it was like living my childhood all over again. The good news is that my brother, Ezra, is pretty amazing and so is Levon. The baby of the family, and only daughter, Mariah, is the spitting image of her dad's mom and sister. She is a tiny thing. She is twenty years old and hasn't grown an inch or gained a pound since eighth grade. We often laugh and say the only thing that has grown on her is her hair. Mariah, her Nanny Osa, and her aunt Quetta all have the same huge mop of hair that is coarse and curly. It makes them all beautiful.

Family resemblance is a funny thing. I look at my children and I wonder how they all came out so very different. They all came from the same gene pool. They have drastically different personalities. I used to say Mark was type A++ with ADD and Levon was type Z-. Mark never stops moving or talking and is very driven, while Levon is slow to get started and seldom talks. I have to go on record as saying Levon has changed since he has grown up. He is very successful and very self-motivated. Mariah is somewhere in between; she talks a lot and loves life to the fullest, but she can be slow to get started, especially if it is something that isn't that much fun. Unique is the way I describe them all. It's funny, though, because Mariah really has a lot of the personality traits of her bonus dad. I'm sure it's because she's lived with him since she was six. They love music, the same kind of funny movies, and love to get into interesting conversations that I'm not sure I know anything about. Side note, I do remember not long after Steven and I got married while we were on vacation with Mariah and Levon, and we decided to have a characture picture drawn. Mariah and I had ours done together and Steven and Levon had theirs done together. It's funny that the artist must have assumed that Steven was Levon's biological dad. It was amazing how much he could make the two of them look alike in that picture.

So where does the third father come in? I have been married twice, so they have two earthly fathers. However, and most importantly, all three of our children have chosen to follow their heavenly Father. While they have genetic looks that tie them to their earthly father, my favorite thing about them is that they very much resemble their heavenly Father. They have spent many years of their lives getting acquainted with Him and have chose to follow Him in their lives.

The Bible says in Psalm 116:5 *"The LORD is gracious and righteous; our God is full of compassion."* Proverbs 30:5 says *"Every word of God is flawless; he is a shield to those who take refuge in him."* 1 Corinthians 14:33 tells us, *"For God is not a God of disorder but of peace."* These are just a few of the descriptions the Bible gives us about what God looks like. There are many more. So who do you look like? Do you look like your earthly father? More importantly, can people see the resemblance to your heavenly Father? Are you close enough to Him to know what He looks like? The Bible is full of detailed descriptions of what He looks like. Check them out today. Enjoy your genetic family traits but work diligently to form the traits of God and you will enjoy a great life.

To Tell the Truth

Confession time.... I don't really watch that much TV. I have a few shows that I watch regularly. Most of them consist of Fox News, The Voice, and yes, the Bachelor and Bachelorette. The last two shows will make some of you stop reading my book right now. That's why this is towards the end of this book.

Steve and I have this great icebreaker we do when we teach a couples small group or class. We ask the couples this question, "Name a television show you love to watch and one you watch for love." As you can imagine, my sports-loving, super-hero-watching husband watches the Bachelor and the Bachelorette for love. He makes it like a fantasy football team. He chooses the top four he thinks will make it to the finale each season and then picks the one contestant that he thinks the Bachelor or Bachelor-ette will pick in the end. I think as long as he can make it a sporting event, he doesn't have to give up his Man-Card to watch it with me. I must admit right here that he is pretty good at picking his line-up for the season on the first night. He's not one hundred percent correct, but he gets a lot right. On the other hand, our daughter, who at the time I'm writing this, is twenty, hates watching these shows. She will occasionally watch them with us, but it almost always is done under protest and with a loud voice of recommending I check my character and morals. In fact, this season I referred to her as sanctimonious Sue. It's not that she is wrong. Yes, there is absolutely nothing Biblical or even the remotest bit edifying about these shows. In fact, the more I watch the more I think I need to probably re-evaluate my choices. Being a pastor and Life-Coach working with couples, I would never recommend a woman, or man for that matter, date twenty-five people of the opposite sex at the same time, or maybe even in a life time. However, I have been known to try and convince Mariah that I'm only watching because I am doing research for what the world is saying about dating and marriage. Can I just add in here that I'm super proud of my daughter who has chosen to follow Christ and His recommendation to choose a husband by following the leading of the Holy Spirit? I'm pretty sure her success rate will be

much higher than that of any of the Bachelors or Bachelor-
ettes. Thank you God for giving us wisdom as we raised
her and by giving us a lot of grace to cover the times we
didn't do things right.

Really, though, there are several things that you can
learn from the Bachelor and Bachelorette. First, many
times on each show you will hear one of the contestants
say they are taking a risk or getting outside of their comfort zone to be on the show. Sometimes when you follow
God, there are situations that you will face in life that will
cause you to have to step outside of your comfort zone or
box to find what God has for you. In the Bible, God used
Esther to save the Jews. In order to do that she had to take
a risk and approach the King without an invitation. Esther
4:11 says, *"All the king's officials and the people of the royal
provinces know that for any man or woman who approaches the
king in the inner court without being summoned the king has
but one law: that they be put to death unless the king extends
the gold scepter to them and spares their lives. But thirty days
have passed since I was called to go to the king."* (NIV)
Second, choosing to do things your way and not follow
God can lead to some unpleasant consequences. The per-
centage of successful couples that meet on the bachelor
and get engaged at the final rose ceremony and live happily ever after is very small. Most don't make it more than
a year after the show. Choosing to do things your own

way guarantees less success than if you follow the plan that God has chosen for you before you were born. Ephesians 2:10 says, "For we are God's handiwork, created in Christ Jesus to do good works, which God prepared in advance for us to do." Finally, life is about choices. The Bachelor and Bachelorette are presented with twenty-five choices of potential spouses. They sort through them looking for the one that feels like the best choice or feels like they have the best connection with. Rarely do they leave the show without choosing someone. I'm sure they are encouraged by the producers of the show to select someone. No doubt there is incredible pressure to follow their feelings. Experience would tell us that our feelings are fickle and will change frequently about the same topic. One of the biggest hindrances to following God is giving your feelings too big a voice. While feelings are definitely a part of how God created us, they were never meant to be the leading or deciding factor in how we live our lives. Listening to the Holy Spirit and making choices that are directed by Him and the Word of God are the ways to ensure success as we make decisions. As you can see, the Bachelor and Bachelorette do provide us with valuable insight it just goes to show that God can use anything as an object lesson for teaching us important truths.

Unwanted Visitor

Growing up as a young child, we lived in the country and my dad raised game birds. For those of you who don't know what game birds are, they are birds like quail, pheasants, Chukars, ducks, geese, and several other varieties I can't remember at this stage of my life. When you have seven different kinds of quail, four different kinds of pheasants, and so on, a lot of grain is needed to feed them. One of the jobs of my brothers and I was to feed and water the birds every day. It takes a pretty good-sized barn to hold the grain, incubators needed to hatch the eggs of the birds, and all the other necessary equipment it takes to be the master game bird raiser that my dad was. One of the biggest drawbacks to feeding the birds was that mice LOVED the grain. Every day I would go out to the barn to get the grain and open the door and mice would dart across the barn floor. Occasionally a mouse would find its way into one of the grain bins. There is just something about the gross little creatures with those ridiculously ugly tails scurrying across the floor that makes me want to faint. Fainting, though, was not an option. If you passed out, one of them might touch you. I always had a fear that one of them would run up my pants leg and then I would DIE!!!!! I learned to bang really loudly on the door before I opened it to let those torturous creatures get to their hiding places before I came in. Even then I was terrified every time I had to go into the barn. This traumatic childhood ritual created a completely irrational fear of mice in me. I was never so glad as I was the day Dad decided to get out of the game bird business. Even though I was retired from the bird feeding business, I maintained my fear and all-out hatred of rodents for the rest of my life. Did I mention that I hate mice? I hate Mickey Mouse, Minnie Mouse, and all rodents in general. I'm completely confident they were not a part of the original creation of the universe created by a loving Father. Clearly they came as part of the curse when Adam and Eve decided to believe Satan instead following the clear directives of God. After all, Satan did come in the form of a snake and snakes eat mice.....I rest my case.

For many years of my life, I have made no bones about the fact that I HATE MICE! If you have been in my life for any amount of time you know I HATE MICE! On one occasion my son, Mark, put a fake mouse in my shoe and I found it when I put it on my foot. Out of shear reflex, I nearly beat that kid to death with that shoe. Momma don't play when it comes to mice! My best friend even got me a birthday card with a glittered mouse on it one year and I shredded it so fast it made her head spin. I HATE MICE!

As an adult, when my parents retired and built a house in the country, I understood that there would always be the possibility of running into a mouse. I was hyper-vigilant about looking for them. I never wanted to see any indicators that mice might have decided to come in the house. Until that one fateful day. Me, my mom, and my two boys were going into Mom's house. Her house had a beautiful glassed sun room along the entire south side of the house. It provided an amazing view of the huge lake my dad had built once they moved on the property. On this sunny day, as we opened the door to the sun room, a mouse ran into the house right under our feet. Well, as you can imagine I was having no part of that. Honestly, my mom was not really digging it either. So we did what all moms do, we assigned the task of getting that mouse out of the sun room to my sons, who at the time, were seven and eleven years old. Mom and I rushed into the other part of the house and barricaded the door to the sun room, making sure the devil mouse couldn't get into the part of the house we were in, and yelled directions to the boys through the glass door. I'm sure that we would have won the America's Funniest Home Video contest that day if we had thought to record the entire event. Those poor boys, armed with brooms and pool cues, directed by two screaming women, chased that mouse around the room for nearly an hour. By some act of God they managed to get the demon to run out of the open door back into the wilderness where he came from. My heart raced for hours following that ordeal.

Why is this story important to you? Well, let me bring this around full circle. Many times we allow unwanted visitors in our lives. Maybe for you the unwanted visitor is fear. Yet God tells us in Isaiah 41:10 *"So do not fear, for I am with you; do not be dismayed, for I am your God. I will strengthen you and help you; I will uphold you with my righteous right hand."* Maybe the unwanted visitor is anger. Again, God tells us in Proverbs 29:11 *"Fools give full vent to their rage, but the wise bring calm in the end."* There are many other unwanted visitors that can try to invade your life. The beautiful part is that no matter what the unwanted visitor is, God has placed in his Word a scripture to help you evict it. We are called to live powerful lives with our hearts fully devoted to God. I encourage you today. Check your heart and see if there are any unwanted visitors. If you find them, don't send a child with a broom or pool cue to fight them, fight them and evict them with the powerful sword of the Spirit. God will empower you to serve those visitors the eviction notice they deserve and give you the power to keep them from returning.

What a Difference A Year or Fifty Make

There really are two kinds of people in the world, people who are older than I and people who are younger than I. Age is a curious thing. When you're a preteen, everyone over twenty seems old to you and people over fifty seem ancient. I remember when I was a young teenager my Uncle Charlie turned forty. Charlie was the youngest child, the only son with five older sisters. To say he was a tad bit spoiled might be one of the biggest understatements of the century! According to my mother, the oldest child in the family, Charlie was pampered and spoiled by everyone. At the time of Charlie's fortieth birthday, I made the astute observation that he had officially reached the status of "wow, he is really old!" Funny how, as I got older, forty seemed younger. Age is one of those things that is the cause for much debate and often hedging the truth. My mother, for instance, was the oldest twenty-nine-year-old you ever met. In fact, my mother was twenty-nine as long as I can remember. She continually turned twenty-nine year after year. So much so that there were several things that were said about her umpteenth twenty-ninth birthday. I would usually say my mom had been lying about her age for so long I didn't think she even knew hold she was. When my nephew, David, was about eight, he asked my mother how old she was on her birth-day, to which my mother promptly replied, "Well, David, I am twenty-nine." David, with a very puzzled look on his face, finally said, "Wow! You are younger than my dad, but you sure don't look like it!" Don't kids just say the darnedest things? I must report that in 2004, after spend-ing a short sixty-seven years on earth, my mother went to live with Jesus at the perfect age of twenty-nine. Since she is currently enjoying every day with Jesus, and because 1 Peter 3:8 says, *"But do not forget this one thing, dear friends: With the Lord a day is like a thousand years, and a thousand years are like a day;"* my mother may have been more right than we all gave her credit for.

Prepare yourselves for the shock of the century. Are you bracing yourself? Close the book for a moment right now and find my picture on the back cover of this book. Do you recognize the very well-preserved, fifty-three-year old? Yes, I have arrived at the age of people who frequently get an AARP card offer in the mail. My first one was enough to make me sit in shock and shed a tear or two. Now when those silly things arrive at my house, my amazing husband, who just happens to be a few years younger than I, politely retrieves them from the mail and promptly places them in the trash before I ever have to see them. I can continue to live in the blissful land of denial. Honestly, crossing the fifty-year mark doesn't look anything like I thought it would. I'm happy to report that my beautiful daughter says, "Mom, you and Steve are not old. Every one of my friends think you are in your early forty'-s." I'll take, and happily embrace, the wisdom of a few brilliant millennials. Yes, I really believe that age is a state of mind. I choose the state of mind that I haven't even hit middle age yet because God says we can have one hundred and twenty years. I plan on claiming every one of them. I have a lot of amazing life yet to live and stories to share.

The year before my fiftieth birthday I began to recognize I was about to join a crowd that I wasn't that excited about joining. As a pastor of a large church, I am one of the oldest people on the staff. In fact, I am old enough to be the mother of many of them. I like to remind them that I would have had to be a teen mom, but it would have been possible. For many months prior to turning fifty, feeling like I had not even touched the beginning of what God had put in my heart to do, I began to question the all-knowing God about His clear understanding of my age. Many mornings when we met for coffee, (I'm confident that God loves coffee too), I would take time to remind Him that I was not getting any younger. Seriously, I had this conversation with him on nearly a daily basis for months. I recognize that telling the Creator of the universe that He was unaware of your age is ridiculous, but for me, I had to hash it out for myself more than for Him. God's response to this repetitive conversation was really helpful in getting unstuck. He showed me a huge battlefield, much what I would imagine the Civil War must have looked like. In it were many dead soldiers I had defeated. He said every time you go back over this issue, it's like you are out on the battlefield making the dead soldiers come alive again so you can fight the battle over and over. No one does that. Sometimes we just have to let defeated enemies remain defeated. What I learned from all of this is that God is fully aware of the number of your days. In fact, Luke 12:7 says, *"Indeed, the very hairs of your head are all numbered."* I'm pretty sure that if God can keep a constant count of the ever-changing number of hairs on my head, He is able to know the number of my days. In the end, I have come to accept that I'm not as young as I used to be, but I can certainly accomplish a lot in whatever the remaining years of my life are. So what will you do with your remaining days? Will you live them to fullest? Will you squeeze every drop of goodness out of them? Will you make every one of them count for the Kingdom? Make a commitment today to live each day to the fullest and receive everything that God has for you. I'll end with this quote, even though I can't find who to attribute it to, "Life is not a journey to the grave with the intention of arriving safely in a pretty and well preserved body, but rather to skid in, broadside, thoroughly used up, totally worn out, loudly proclaiming -- WOW-- what a ride!"

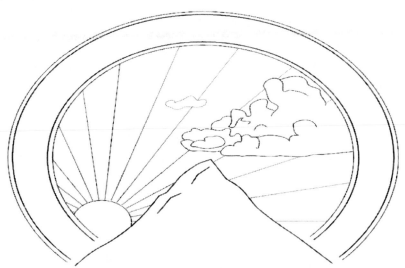

WHAT ARE YOU LEAVING BEHIND?

In my adult life I have moved five times and I have learned that very often you find yourself with way more stuff than you really are interested in taking with you to the next place. Packing up and going through everything is quite the chore. One of my first moves came in the form of leaving a two-bedroom mobile home and moving into my first actual house. We called moving it into a house without wheels. I had dreamed of the day when I would move into a "real" house. After living in an eight-hundred and forty-square feet home for twelve years, I felt like I was being released from a twelve-year prison sentence. I was actually going to have room to spread out. I envisioned room to put everything away and room to spare. I could be heard singing the theme song to "The Jeffersons" television show for days before the move. It was going to be glorious. I had dreamed of this day for years! No more mobile home living for this girl. We decided to put the house up for sale. My expectations were low. Who would actually want this place. At the encouraging of my best friend, I finally did it. I listed the house for sale. It came as total amazement to me. Someone actually was interested in buying the place I was anxiously awaiting leaving. One man's trash is another man's treasure was how I felt about it. All of a sudden we had sold our home. Here's the catch, we had only a week to move. Who knew it was going to go that fast? Holy smoke, I was shocked really. Now I find myself in the place of having to hurry and find us a new place to live. As you can see, my expectations were far exceeded. After a couple of days of looking, I found our new home. We were going to be renting a seventeen hundred square foot home. It was amazing, except for what the people who moved out had left. Imagine with me, if you will, a house with three spacious bedrooms, a very large living room, two bathrooms, a huge fenced back yard completed by a covered car-port. Those are the amazing parts of the house. So much space I barely knew what to do with it. With all that goodness, came dog hair. Tons and tons of black dog hair. I was completely convinced that the renter who lived there before me was leaving with a large bald dog who used to have black hair. So I now have four days to pack my home, clean the dog hair out of the new house, and move on up to the south side. As you can imagine, my best friend, my mom, and I spent at least two days cleaning this mess. That left me very little time to pack my own house. I was only left with the option of having my dad, my husband, and his best friend to pack up our house...........REALLY BAD IDEA. When you are short on time, you do what you have to do. Their idea of packing was not my idea of packing. They thought, here's a drawer, here's a box, DUMP! No need to label it, we will just figure it out as get to the next place. This is what nightmares are made of. Packing was easy for them, unpacking was going to take weeks for me. It was crazy, but I was getting a big ol' house without wheels.

When I went back to clean the mobile home we were moving out of, I found many things they thought we should leave behind. Trust me, you don't really know what you can collect and cram in eight hundred and forty square feet until you move. I found broken things, old things, but the thing I found most of were small, two inch pieces of plastic sacks. Because I know that you are asking what is the meaning behind the plastic sack pieces, I will interject a funny story about one of my sons. Kids do some of the craziest things. Well, my son, who will remain nameless for this story, was a finger sucker. No, he didn't suck his thumb, he sucked the index and second finger on his left hand. While this is not all that uncommon, the other part of what he did is. While sucking his finger, he loved to play with the top of his disposable diaper. Something about that plastic piece of his diaper was soothing to him. It was the funniest thing. I tried everything I could think of to get him to quit. I dressed him in overalls that covered his diaper, but no, he would still find a way to get to part of his diaper. I tried putting him in one-piece pajamas with a zipper and snap at the top. I would awaken in the morning to find that he had managed to unzip the pajamas so he could rub his fingers on the top of his diaper. I had finally resolved that when he no longer needed diapers this problem would naturally resolve itself. I was wrong! A determined child discovered that plastic bags had a very similar feel to his diaper. Seriously, he couldn't go to sleep without rubbing the top of his diaper between his fingers. It was the only way he would be soothed. It was not something that he was going to give up that easily. Diapers were traded in for pieces of a plastic sack which he lovingly referred to as his "piece of diapy." Back to cleaning the mobile home. There were thousands of pieces of plastic sack all over our house. They were behind every piece of furniture, hundreds behind his bed, and they were even found behind the washer and dryer. I have no explanation for how they got there. The good news is that when we left the mobile home, my son left his "piece of diapy" there too.

All too often in our life we pick up things that unintentionally stay with us for way to long. Belief systems, habits, and even fears somehow find a way to take up residence in our lives and sometimes without even knowing it, become a hindrance in our lives. While my now adult son no longer needs a "piece of diapy" in his life, I'm sure if you asked him, he would tell you there are other things that he would like to leave behind. In Hebrews 12:1, Paul discusses this very condition that plagues so many people. *"Therefore, since we are surrounded by such a great cloud of witnesses, let us throw off everything that hinders and the sin that so easily entangles. And let us run with perseverance the race marked out for us."* What are the things in your life that you need to leave behind? Are you willing to lay down those things that keep you from living the life the God has prepared for you? It's not always easy, and many times it takes serious thought and practice to leave them behind, but the payoff is always worth it. Just remember my mom's life verse Philippians 4:13 "I can do all this through him who gives me strength." It just might make your life even better.

What Are You Picking Up

Dogs are a standard in our house. As an adult I have always had a dog. We usually have more than one. At one time we found ourselves with four. In fact, my husband and I have written a book about the things God taught us as we walked our dogs. It's a great book called Walking With ~~Dog~~ God. You can find it on our website at www.bridgebuildermm.org/resources. Enough of the shameless plug. One of the things I have noticed with dogs is that there is shedding. Vacuuming is a frequent activity in our house. It just comes with the territory of being a dog owner.

I read an article several months ago that said that people who wear socks to bed actually sleep better. The older I get the more I began to notice that my feet got cold at night, so I decided to start wearing socks to bed. I must confess that it has helped me sleep better. If you have trouble sleeping, you just might try wearing socks to bed. A good night's sleep helps everyone.

I'm sure by now you are wondering what these two seemingly unrelated stories have to do with each other. I will bring them together and hopefully create a beautiful picture. When I get out of bed in the morning, I just run around the house in my sock feet. I find that by the time I am ready to take my shower and get ready for the day, my socks are occasionally adorned with dog hair. UGH! There is no such thing as wearing the socks to bed the next night without washing them first. The crazy thing is, I wasn't planning to get them covered in dog hair. I wasn't trying to get them too dirty to wear a second time. I just picked up the dog hair as I went about my normal morning activities. This sometimes happens with offense. Going through our normal daily activities we will have the opportunity to take offense about one thing or sometimes many things. It's not that we set out intending to be offended, it just happens as we encounter people. Offense is an enemy of relationship. The devil likes nothing more than to get someone in a place where they are offended and cause damage to a relationship. Unlike the dog hair on my socks, offense is something that we make a decision to pick up. We choose to allow ourselves to be offended. I understand that often times we do it without conscious thought but none the less, we choose to take it. Jesus said, in John 14:27, *"Peace I leave with you; My [own] peace I now give and bequeath to you...[Stop allowing yourselves to be agitated and disturbed; and do not permit yourselves to be fearful and intimidated and cowardly and unsettled]"* AMP I think this is a great reminder. While it doesn't necessarily use the word offended, I think we could easily add it to the text and have a clear understanding of how we choose to pick up offense. The first part of that verse is very important in that it reveals to us that Jesus has given us everything we need. He has left us His peace. We can choose not to be offended. We can choose to leave the offense laying where we found it. Just this simple thoughtful process could actually make our lives so much easier. Today I challenge you, choose to leave the offense where you found it. Don't pick it up. Walk in the peace that Jesus died for you to have. It will make your life so much better. It may not be easy, but it is worth every effort you make. The payoff is huge.

WHAT IF......

For years my husband, Steven, and I have played this game. We call it "what if we won the lottery?" We dream of what we would do with the amazing winnings. We start off with the fact that we would take a one-time pay out. Heck, if we win that much money we figure that we would be better stewards of it than the lottery people paying us out over the years. We would then portion out the tithe, ten percent of the gross. That would really make our pastor happy, as he would get to figure out what to do with a huge sum of money. We then decided what percent of it we would invest so we would have money to live comfortably for the rest of our lives. Now that's when the fun part starts! We often talk about how we could help our children. Next comes Steven's mom. We would also want to help our siblings. What would their lives look like if they didn't have a house payment? Next comes the Bridge Builder Marriage Retreat Center, as well as money to fund our ministry. There are also a group of ministries and friends that we would love to bless with some money. Finally, we would set up a bunch of foundations that would help people who needed it over time. This is a super fun game. You see, we have had the privilege of being generous in our lives and we know the joy it brings when we get to share what God has given us with other people and seeing lives impacted by paying off someone's bills, paying their rent, or maybe just giving them money for a date night. We understand what it is like to live out Acts 20:35, *"it is more blessed to give than to receive."*

Playing "What if we won the lottery," is really fun, but it doesn't really change anything for us or for anyone else. What it does do is help demonstrate the idea of what would I do if money were not a problem. Many times we have things that God has put in our hearts to do, but we never even really entertain the idea of doing them because we don't feel like we have the money to make it happen. Maybe we decide we can't do the 'what if' things in our dreams because we don't think we know where to start, we are afraid of failing, or maybe we are afraid of succeeding. There are many reasons people don't step out to make their dreams a reality. What is yours?

In 2003 Steven and I met online. I was living in a small town in western Oklahoma with 250 other people and Steven was living in Minneapolis, Minnesota, 2.5 million people. Our lives couldn't have been more different. I had just come out of a twenty-year failed marriage and he had never been married. I had three kids, he had none, and despite all of this God brought us together. We had both decided to take the risk of trying to find someone outside our town and we found each other. Then Steven decided to leave everything he knew, family, friends, job, and church, and move south nine hundred miles to a very small farm community to marry someone completely different. Big risk, yes, but the pay-off has been amazing? I have a friend who always tells me, "I hate change." Well, change isn't easy for most people. Big changes are even terrifying at times. However, choosing to stay with the status quo may just prevent you from missing the most amazing things in life. Sometimes in life we just have to make changes and do it afraid.

I wonder what are the things you are thinking 'what if' about. For us, one of the what ifs we faced after Steven gave up everything to move to my village with me was to follow a dream that God had placed in our hearts to do marriage ministry. The dream first led me down a path to give up a cushy nursing career to become an administrative assistance at a church. Can you say 'big pay cut?' Next it involved us going to Beulah, North Dakota to a church conference. We didn't know who was preaching and I had to get out the map to figure out where Beulah even was. Then we took a risk of staying in the home of people we had never met before for a week. This act of bravery was what we needed to really launch us out into our marriage ministry and publishing our first book. Later we took another huge step and decided that Steven would leave a full-time job and do ministry full time without a guaranteed salary each month. Believe me, that's a big step to take in the 'what if' game. We gave up over sixty-five percent of our total income and dared to follow a dream God had put in our hearts. We always felt we had to follow the scripture in Psalm 37:23 *"The steps of a good man are ordered by the LORD: and he delighteth in his way" (KJV)*. Looking back, we now see that God's hand was on what we were doing, yet it was hard at times, and yes, there were times when we weren't sure how we were going to pay the bills, but in those times, we found God was faithful. In years past we have seen many marriages restored, marriages begun with a solid foundation, and children's lives saved because their parents decided not to cut and run when the going got tough.

Again, I ask, what are the things in your heart that you are saying 'what if' about? 'What if' you were brave? 'What if' you decided to follow the dreams in your heart? '

What if' you took a risk? 'What if' you got to live the life you always wanted? I want to challenge you. Take a chance. Make a change and see what amazing things God can do in your life. Maybe you have to do it afraid, but I believe you can do it. Get off the sidelines and get into the game! No more 'what ifs.' No more fear, nothing but faith from here on out. Just do it. I know you can. I promise you might just take the ride of your life and you might just change the world.

In Conclusion

One of my favorite sayings is, "Life is a journey, just keep moving." Time moves on whether we want it to or not. I didn't really ever plan to be fifty-three, but if you live long enough it happens to everyone. Looking back at the stories of my life, I find that there were so many times when God's hand was on my life, even when I didn't know Him or recognize Him. God has been with me every day, at every moment, and when I choose to allow Him, He will fill all the parts of my life with good things. He will even take the things in my life that I think are bad and turn them around and make them something I wouldn't trade for the world. I have walked through some really fun and silly times, but I have also walked through tough ones. The death of both my parents, a huge family fight over a piece of family property, the years of addiction to drugs that my boys struggled with, and even the end of a twenty-year marriage. You can just say thank you now that I didn't add those times to the book, it would have been way less funny. Even in those times, God was with me and the stories that came out of them were treasures to me. I have learned through the years that God is faithful, but above all God is love. The Bible says "Whoever does not love does not know God, because God is love." 1 John 4:9 I have learned to recognize this in every situation. There is a country western song that says, "Thank God for unanswered prayers." Yes, even in the times when I didn't see God moving in a situation that I really wanted Him to, I know that He was working on my behalf. I recognize now that even prayers that I felt went unanswered were God's blessing to me.

What do the next forty or even fifty years of my life hold, I truly have no idea! But I do know this one thing, God will be with me on the journey and He will never leave me. He made that promise to me in Deuteronomy 31:6, "Be strong and courageous. Do not be afraid or terrified because of them, for the LORD your God goes with you; he will never leave you nor forsake you." I can honestly say I am very excited about what's next and what God will show me in the future. I still have a lot of plans I want to see come to pass. I want to learn how to love people better because they are God's favorite thing. I want to know more about who God is. The youth pastor at my church, Levi Carter, and I were having a conversation one day and we were discussing the passage of scripture in Revelations where it talks about the beings around the throne of God who would be at the throne day and night saying, "Holy, holy, holy is the Lord God Almighty, who was, and is, and is to come." Revelations 4:8. My thought was "that's a really long time to spend doing the same thing." I personally thought that I would rather enjoy exploring all the parts of heaven, but Levi said something that changed everything about how I viewed that scripture and how I view God. He said, "I just think that God has so many things about Him that we have never discovered. Each time He reveals something new to the beings, they and the twenty-four elders are so overwhelmed by the new part of God that they discovered they can't help but fall on their faces and worship Him more." I loved that and those thoughts have really changed the way I see God. God has so much to show us about Himself. I think of it like a diamond which has many facets. Each facet is so different than the one before it. I have found, over time, that God is more than happy to reveal a new facet of Himself to me every day. I now approach every morning with God, well really, every day, with God with the expectation of seeing a new part of God I have never experienced before. In fact, as I wrote this book, I discovered so many times in the past that God had revealed Himself to me in ways I didn't know existed until I went back to remember them. Because of this approach to my life and God's hand in it, I look forward to the opportunity to spend fifty years or more learning more about the Creator of the universe who longs to spend every moment of every day with me.

What will your story say? What ways will you discover something about God you don't yet know? Whether from your past, your present, or your future, God has so much to show you. He is along for the journey of your life to write the most amazing story ever told, but He can't do it without you. In order for the story to be told, you have to do the telling. The Bible tells us, *"And they overcame him because of the blood of the Lamb and because of the word of their testimony."* Revelation 12:11a (NASB) My hope is that this book has been a pleasure for you to read, but more that, it has caused you to take a new look at who God is in your life. Maybe it has inspired you to take a look back and see where God's fingerprints were but you just missed them. Most of all, I hope that it gives you excitement as you look at your future. Join me on the adventure of a lifetime to discover and share the treasures you can find as we live our lives with "mornings well spent."

Melisa Zimmerman is the co-founder of Bridge Builder Marriage Ministry, which is dedicated to helping couples have a life-giving marriage. She is an ordained minister currently on staff at Victory Church in Oklahoma City, a Life Coach, speaker, writer and storyteller. Melisa is a woman who wears many hats. She has spoken at conferences and led women's groups for many years and has a passion to see people live the blessed life God designed for them. She and her husband, Steven, live in Yukon, Oklahoma and enjoy spending time with their children and grandchildren.

CPSIA information can be obtained
at www.ICGtesting.com
Printed in the USA
FFOW02n1528170718
47405114-50600FF

9 780982 676554